# HOMELANDS AND HEARTLANDS

Dedicated to Peter who sadly did not live to see his book in print. With loving thanks for his ability to listen and his quiet determination to see this project fulfilled.

# Homelands

## and

# Heartlands

*Forgotten Victims of World War II*

by

## Peter Cowles

ROUNDHAY PARK PRESS

Copyright © Marika Cowles 2004
Published posthumously
First published in 2004 by Roundhay Park Press
22 Ayresome Terrace
Leeds LS8 1BJ

Distributed by Gazelle Book Services Limited
Hightown, White Cross Mills, South Rd, Lancaster
England LA1 4XS

British Library Cataloguing in Publication Data
A catalogue record for this book is available from the British
Library

ISBN 0-9546872-0-5

Typeset by Amolibros, Milverton, Somerset
This book production has been managed by Amolibros
Printed and bound by Advance Book Printing, Oxford, England

## Foreword

THE IDEA FOR writing this book came to me gradually. I listened, over a period of several years, to the stories told by my partner's parents, of their early lives in Hungary, and what happened to them and their families during and following the Second World War. This was a slow and difficult process for me, since they do not speak English, and my German is limited.

The more I listened, the more I became enthralled. They spoke of life-threatening events with little anger or resentment. It was just what happened to them, and they could have neither influenced nor controlled events. I started taking notes to put their stories on paper. Of course their recollection of events of fifty years and more ago has to be taken on trust, but I am sure that the basic facts are correct.

I needed to put their stories into an historical context, which meant some more formal research. Since my main sources were written in German that also took some time.

The end result is a story based on the history of German settlement in Hungary, but much more on the families' own experiences, with a little poetic licence from me, where I could not fill gaps in the story from their recollections. Their stories will be typical of many refugees, but, because of resentment towards Germans generally in the period after the Second World War, and maintained by some even now, their stories have been little documented.

*Peter Cowles*

# Sources for historical information

*Die Geschichte der Gemeinde Elek in Ungarn*
(The History of the District of Elek in Hungary)
Johann Stöckl and Franz Brandt

*Geschichte der Donauschwaben*
(History of the Danube Swabians)
Josef Volkmar Senz

"History of German Settlements in Southern Hungary"
(Internet article by Sue Clarkson for www.genealogy.com)

ELEK FAMILIES

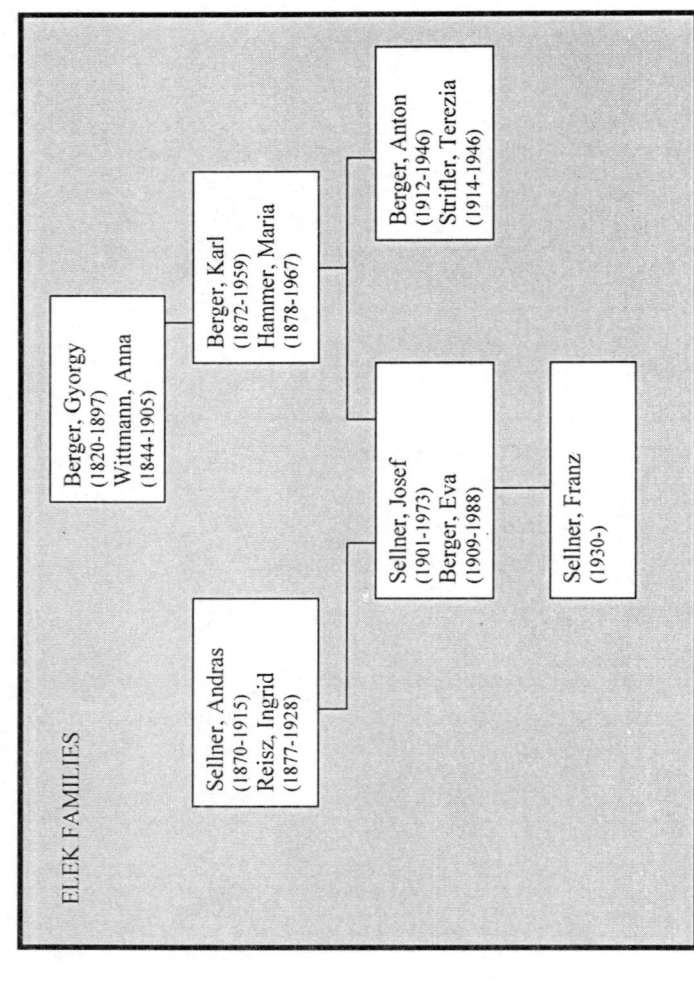

Berger, Gyorgy
(1820-1897)
Wittmann, Anna
(1844-1905)

Berger, Karl
(1872-1959)
Hammer, Maria
(1878-1967)

Berger, Anton
(1912-1946)
Strifler, Terezia
(1914-1946)

Sellner, Andras
(1870-1915)
Reisz, Ingrid
(1877-1928)

Sellner, Josef
(1901-1973)
Berger, Eva
(1909-1988)

Sellner, Franz
(1930-)

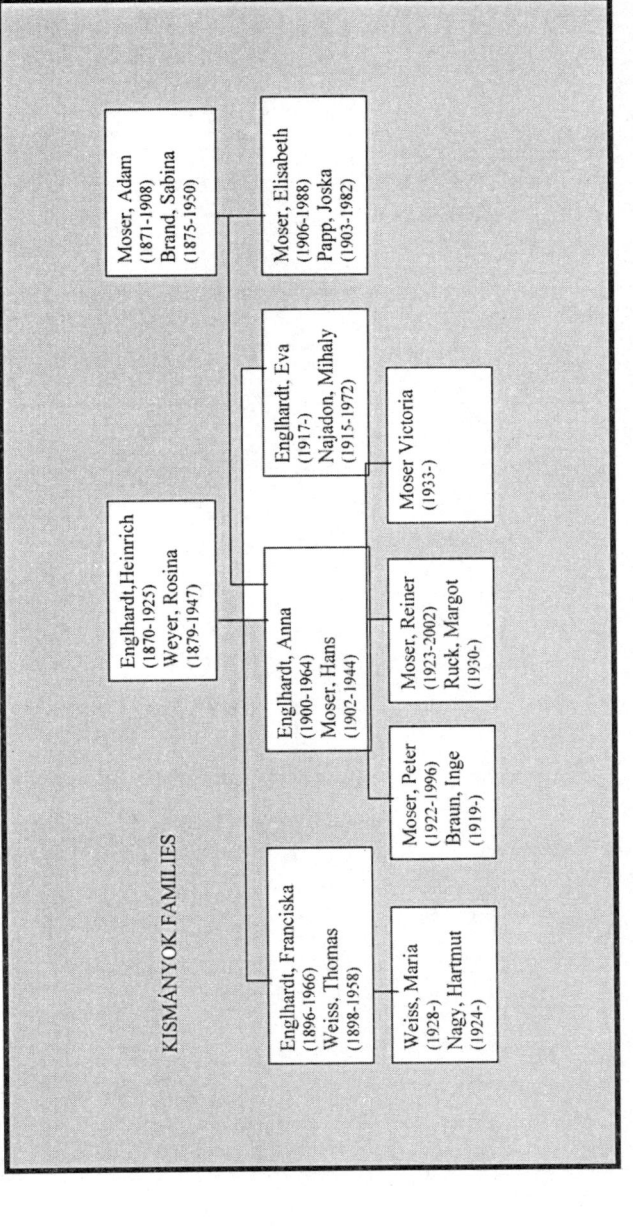

KISMÁNYOK FAMILIES

Moser, Adam
(1871-1908)
Brand, Sabina
(1875-1950)

Moser, Elisabeth
(1906-1988)
Papp, Joska
(1903-1982)

Englhardt, Heinrich
(1870-1925)
Weyer, Rosina
(1879-1947)

Englhardt, Eva
(1917-)
Najadon, Mihaly
(1915-1972)

Moser Victoria
(1933-)

Englhardt, Anna
(1900-1964)
Moser, Hans
(1902-1944)

Moser, Reiner
(1923-2002)
Ruck, Margot
(1930-)

Moser, Peter
(1922-1996)
Braun, Inge
(1919-)

Englhardt, Franciska
(1896-1966)
Weiss, Thomas
(1898-1958)

Weiss, Maria
(1928-)
Nagy, Hartmut
(1924-)

FRANZ LOOKED OUT across the fields. It was hot in September's late evening sunshine. His parents had left, and the dusty farmyard seemed strangely quiet. But the five cows had been left behind, and they were demanding attention. They had had no water all day, and needed to be milked. It wouldn't take long, so he walked back through the deserted farmyard to the cowshed. Once inside he worked quickly to get water from the pump just outside the door, and filled the trough at the end of the stall. When the cows had drunk enough he hand-milked them one by one to relieve their bulging udders. It was work he had done hundreds of times before even though he was only thirteen, and still had some growing to do. He had been born at the farm, and had helped with the work there for as long as he could remember.

Once he had completed his task, he set off across the fields to the neighbour's farm, a mile to the south-west, towards the village of Elek, where he knew his parents would be waiting. Better keep off the track, just in case. But this was the Puszta, the great plain of Hungary, flat for as far as the eye could see in every direction, and, apart from the occasional tree or farmhouse, this farmland offered little chance to stay out of sight. He heard the sound of the motor some way behind him, and started to run. He heard the crack of the tank's gun, which startled him, and he fell headlong forwards in the grass. As he fell the shell crashed into the ground twenty yards ahead of him, and he was showered with earth and pieces of flying metal. He put his hand to his forehead and felt the wet blood. He lay there expecting another shell, but the tank must have changed course, and he heard the sound of the motor grow fainter and fade away. He slowly stood up and looked around. Still nothing moved. The cut on his head didn't hurt much and the blood was just a trickle. He scurried in a crouched position across the fields to the neighbour's farm, from where his father and mother watched his approach, yet not daring to show themselves until he was in the yard. His mother, Eva, grabbed his arm and took him to the tap in the yard where she quickly poured water on his wound. She was relieved to see that it wasn't a deep cut, and he soon had a rough bandage wrapped around his head, so that he looked like a Red Indian brave. Josef, his father, shouted at him. He had never been averse to beating his son, and only refrained now because of the wound.

"Why did you go back? You could easily have been killed."

"The cows needed water and milking."

"Haven't you got a brain in your head? We're in the middle of a war, and you worry about the cows!"

ॐ

It was indeed a war, and right now they were living on the front line. It was September 1944 and the tanks were part of the Russian invading army. When it had first entered the war, Hungary had fought on the German side, as had Rumania. In August 1944, when faced with the massed Russian army on its eastern borders, the Rumanians changed sides to fight with the Russians, rather than take further losses and incur even greater destruction. The German forces, together with what was left of the Hungarian army, had launched a counter-attack, and for fourteen days the Hungarian village of Elek was on the front line. Many of the inhabitants of the village centre had fled to avoid the fighting, and, of those who remained, all the young girls and women were in hiding. The Germans had appropriated all the horses from the farms, mainly to avoid them falling into the hands of the Russians. Some of the farmers outside the village had stayed at or near their farms, including Josef and his wife Eva, and some of their neighbours.

Josef Sellner's farm was over three miles north-east of Elek, an hour's walk away. In normal times Franz had had to walk there and back each day to go to school, and it took him almost an hour each way. He was glad that his grandfather had his farmhouse right in the village, so that he could stay there when there was a midday break.

Two days later the fighting moved further south towards the village. Josef and Eva decided to stay with their neighbours until they felt it was safe to return home. Franz, never much one for taking advice or instructions, hence the frequent beatings by his father, decided to go back to the farm in order to look after the cows. Neither Josef nor Eva knew where he had gone. They thought he had gone to his grandparents in the village. They weren't going to make the dangerous journey across open fields to find out.

Franz made himself comfortable, ate from the vast store of food from the recent harvest, and decided to sleep in his parents' bedroom, which was much bigger and more comfortable than was his own bedroom. The farmhouse was traditional in its layout. There were three rooms in a line, decreasing in size one to the next. The large living room and kitchen were at one end, then the bedroom used by his mother and father, and his own small room, at the other end. The house was single-storey, but there was access to a large loft space, where crops were stored to be eaten during the long winters. There were two beds, one either side of his parents' room, so he chose the one he liked the best.

He was woken in the morning by the shouting of his father in the yard outside. He opened his eyes and was surprised to see a gaping hole in the roof over the other bed in the room, which was covered in rubble. His bed was covered with fruit and vegetables, which had fallen through the collapsed ceiling from the loft above where they had been stored. At least he had chosen the right bed in which to sleep! He was unhurt, and even the shell bursting through the roof had not woken him! From then on, Franz decided he had better stick with his parents.

Two days later the Russians launched a massive attack, and the German and Hungarian forces were pushed back to the west. Life returned to something approaching normal, apart from the fact that a few Russian soldiers were left to keep order.

## Chapter One

FRANZ AND HIS family lived near the village of Elek almost on the Rumanian border, but they spoke German as their first language, although they could also speak Hungarian. About 6,000 of the village's 9,000 or so inhabitants did the same. Of the remainder about 2,000 spoke Hungarian, and most of the rest Rumanian, apart from a few Serbs. Although everyone was taught in Hungarian at school, there was at least one lesson each week, which although not a language lesson, was taught to all the class in German, and another in Rumanian, so that there was recognition of the ethnic mix of the local population. The reasons for this mix of population were historical, and went back several hundred years.

A number of German speakers had arrived in what was to become Hungary as early as the tenth century. These were mainly craftsmen and builders who settled in the towns. In 1526 at the battle of Mohács, which is in modern-day southern Hungary not far from the River Danube, the Ottoman army invading from the south-east inflicted a crushing defeat on the Hungarian forces, and the Hungarian King Louis II was killed. From then until the end of the seventeenth century two-thirds of Hungary was under Turkish occupation. The remaining parts of the north came under the control of the Habsburg Kings, ruling from their Court in Vienna.

It was impossible for the Hungarian inhabitants in the areas occupied by the Turks to live a normal existence. Many of them were killed, or taken away into slavery. Others were made to work for the Turks as slave labour, and many more fled to the north. There was extensive depopulation, most of the trees were chopped down, and the farmland became a wasteland. The great plain of the south-east became a boggy marsh, with isolated settlements on islands of drier land.

For over 170 years there were frequent battles as the Hungarians, backed by the Habsburgs, tried to drive the Turks out. It wasn't until the late seventeenth century that the Habsburg armies became strong enough to expel the Ottomans. Prince Eugen was put in command of the army, and with the help of his generals, notably the Count of Mercy, took on the Turkish forces. In a series of battles the Ottomans were pushed back, culminating in a major battle at Zenta in September 1697, where the Turkish army was smashed. The Ottomans were forced to negotiate a truce, and by the treaty of Karlowitz in 1699, had to cede Hungary to the Habsburgs. Prince Eugen knew that the truce was fragile. He pressed his army on southwards into what had formerly been parts of Croatia, Serbia, and Slovenia, so that the southern boundary could be defined as the River Danube. The problem with this boundary was its distance from the main populated parts of Hungary, and the length of the lines of supply for the armies.

The Habsburg King was delighted with the expulsion of the Turks, and the gaining of new lands for the Empire. A commission was set up in order to allow claimants to the recaptured lands to prove their claims. Since the Turks had been in control for over 170 years it proved difficult for more than a handful of Hungarians to establish rightful claims. The Catholic Church was able to claim some lands, but large parts of southern Hungary reverted to Crown ownership. This enabled the King to grant large estates of land to his successful generals, including Prince Eugen and the Count of Mercy. Other estates were granted to favoured court officials. Many of the soldiers who had fought against the Turks settled in the south, and helped to dig the first ditches and canals to start draining the marshlands.

If the native Magyar Hungarians thought salvation had arrived as a result of the treaty of Karlowitz, they were to be badly disappointed initially. The Habsburg armies occupied southern Hungary. They persecuted the Hungarians, particularly the Protestants. The remaining Hungarians in the south changed from being Turkish slaves to serfdom under the new landowners.

The new landed estates were referred to as Pusztas—confusing, because that was also the name used for the great southern plain. Most of the estates were laid out along similar lines, with the centre of each estate comprising a square of buildings around an open courtyard. One section of the buildings would be for the employees. They were dependent on the landowner for work, accommodation, and food. Living conditions were bad, often with two families living in one room.

The oppressive Habsburg occupation led to a rebellion by the Hungarians. Eventually in 1711 the treaty of Szatmar set up separate legal and administrative systems for Hungary within the Habsburg Empire. That may have relieved the oppression, but did little for the poverty endured by Hungarians in the rural south. Some remnants of the estate way of life continued up to the beginning of the First World War in 1914.

In 1711 huge parts of Hungary were still wastelands. Re-building needed some impetus, and that meant many more people. Immediately after the treaty of Szatmar the Habsburg King, Karl III, called upon Catholic-controlled districts of Germany to allow some of their subjects to emigrate to Hungary. This policy had several intentions: first, to try to establish Catholicism amongst the predominantly Protestant population; second, to enable the nobles who owned the land to have tenant farmers who would pay rent; third, to convert the wasteland into productive farmland. And last, but not least, to increase tax receipts for the Empire following successful re-population.

As a result between 14,000 and 16,000 emigrants went to Hungary in the early eighteenth century, mostly from southern Germany. They were opportunists who anticipated taking over established farms, which they could soon put right, and make profitable. They were in for a shock. Once they saw the devastated villages and wet marshlands of the Puszta most of these settlers quickly returned to Germany.

From 1718 onwards a more determined kind of settler began to arrive. They made enquiries to find out if they would be able to find work or land to farm in Hungary, and what they would encounter when they arrived. Rules were made that they had to settle their affairs in Germany before leaving. They had to pay between two and ten per cent (depending on the rules of the places from which they left) of their personal wealth as a "leaving tax", and they had to have at least the equivalent of 200 Hungarian forints to enable them to set up and survive on arrival.

For many this was an attractive proposition. Large parts of Germany had been devastated by the war of Spanish Succession. The emigrants wanted to be free of political and religious persecution, although for many years only Catholics were to be allowed to settle in the new territories. That was the official position, but in fact landowners were so keen to have immigrants that they overlooked this rule, particularly in the south-west of Hungary. If the emigrants could raise the money they could buy themselves from their masters and escape serfdom to become free men, with the probability of renting or even owning their own farms. The German inheritance laws meant only one child could inherit. Other sons often worked as farm labourers, either for their brothers or for other farmers. Some areas of Germany, particularly Franken, had become over-populated. For 200 forints prospective settlers could have land to farm, help to build a house, and enough stock to make a new start, together with the promise of up to fifteen years' tax-free earnings for craftsmen, and ten years for farmers. This was enough to make many decide to take the opportunity. Although they knew they were moving to a country where a different language was spoken they would remain within the Habsburg Empire. An analogy could be made with English settlers moving to Wales, after Welsh independence was finally removed.

The first main wave of settlers, about 15,000 in number, arrived in the period from 1718 to 1737. They came from all over Germany, but most were from the southern areas. Despite their speaking a number of different local German dialects, the Hungarians called them all "Swabians", though this actually refers to only one area of southern Germany. In future all the German settlers in southern Hungary would become known as the Danube Swabians. There were even immigrants from parts of Spain and Italy, but it appears they died of disease or returned to their home countries, because no evidence of their families remains in Hungary.

Many of the Germans made their way to the town of Ulm in southern Germany, which is situated on the Danube. They made crude wooden rafts and floated, or paddled them down the Danube to Vienna. Here they registered for a land allocation before carrying on to Hungary. Sometimes they had horses to pull the rafts along. There were so many of these craft floating down the Danube from Ulm that they earned the nickname "Ulm barges". The journey took five to six weeks, as far as Buda. These Germans either went to existing villages or to set up new settlements. Many did not go to their allocated destinations. Agents of landowners were sent to the main places of disembarkation on the Danube to try to persuade the settlers to change their destinations, offering better terms than they had been given in Vienna.

Often the wood from their "Ulm Barges" was used to construct their first houses. Many of the new settlements were carefully planned on a grid system, particularly on the flat plain of the Danube in the south and east of the country, in the area known as the Puszta, where there were few natural obstacles to such a layout. Usually, wide streets were constructed at right angles to each other, with the church at the centre of the settlement. Houses were built at right angles to the street, with living accommodation next to the street, followed by storage, and then covered quarters for the animals.

Many of the first wave of settlers didn't survive. Diseases such as plague and cholera caused most deaths, but there were also continuing raids from the south by the Turks.

A second wave of about 75,000 settlers arrived in the period from 1744 to 1772. They had to rebuild many of the earlier settlements and re-establish the farms. The final wave of about 60,000 German settlers came from 1782 to 1787, and they were able to reap the benefits from the hardships endured by their predecessors in the earlier immigrations. The official rule of "Catholics Only" was abolished for this final group of settlers. Thus, during the eighteenth century, hundreds of German-speaking Communities were established over a wide area of southern Hungary. Most native Hungarians were against the German immigration, and resented the newcomers enjoying better status than they themselves could achieve.

In the south-east much of the land had been totally devastated, was far away from the main centres of population, and had been largely unoccupied for most of the period of Turkish occupation. The nobles to whom the Habsburgs had given land further to the north did not show much interest in this area, which meant that land was available to purchase, instead of for rent, to those of the settlers who arrived with more money than usual, which some did.

Elek had been an established settlement in the centre of the great plain several centuries before, but had become virtually deserted during the Turkish occupation. The larger town of Gyula, just to the east, had an ancient fortress, and was more easily defendable. When the first of the new settlers arrived in the Elek area in the 1720s they found a flat marsh, with few signs of the original village. The new village was constructed to the accepted planned layout, with wide roads intersecting at right angles on a grid system. If you visit Elek today you will see that the village retains this layout of mostly single-storey houses lining pleasant, for the most part straight, streets. The Church records show that the first group of German immigrants arrived in 1724, with lesser groups coming in 1725 and 1726, making about 300 in total. According to those records, the first families to settle in Elek came from the area to the east of Wurzburg in Germany. There is a Sellner family recorded as coming from the village of Gerolzhofen, in that area, being in Elek in the 1730s. Although it is not possible to show the family descent through to Franz from those settlers, it is very likely that they were his ancestors. The origin of Eva's family, the Bergers is unclear, since they first appear in Elek church records in a marriage in 1773. It could be that the first "Berger" arrived in the second or third wave of settlers, but it is also possible that the Bergers arrived earlier to settle in one of the other villages near to Elek, and the first Berger in Elek moved to the village following his marriage. There are records in the neighbouring village of St Martin showing the name Berger occurring from the 1730s. The family line can be traced from the 1773 marriage clearly down to Eva.

The environment was very unhealthy. The drinking water was bad, so that diseases such as cholera and the plague occurred regularly. Many inhabitants tried not to drink too much water. It is no accident that one of the first crops to be planted was of vines, and remnants of those first vineyards can still be found close to the centre of Elek, and in other villages nearby. On the edges of these villages there are still holes in the ground containing water, evidence of where earth was dug and taken to fill in the boggy ground on the farms. The tasks of building farms, creating land suitable for crops, and producing enough for survival were very hard, and few of the first settlers lived to enjoy the fruits of their labours. In 1739 there was a plague epidemic, which killed 148 inhabitants, around half the population of Elek.

In 1744, a further wave of immigrants arrived from Germany. Life was a little easier for them, since their predecessors had done a lot of the major work. Once drained, the soil proved to be excellent for most crops, and the village became quite prosperous.

The area is comprised of a low lying flat plain. In wet years the water table rises quickly and many houses have flooded cellars. Summers are hot and sticky, with temperatures often over thirty-five degrees. In winter it can be twenty or twenty-five degrees below zero. Wheat can be harvested from June onwards.

There were cholera epidemics in 1831 and 1873, the latter killing 230 inhabitants, and it wasn't until 1894, when the first artesian well was sunk next to the church in the centre of the village, that Elek at last had safe drinking water.

Although the first settlers had built a church in 1733 and attracted a minister the following year, part of whose duties involved keeping records of the population, it is not easy to trace antecedents back to these early immigrants. The minister recorded births, marriages, and deaths, but few of the early inhabitants could read or write. The minister would write down the surname as he heard it, and if it wasn't common, and he didn't know otherwise, if he got it wrong there was usually no one to correct the mistake. Another problem with the church records was caused by the changes in ministers. Sometimes they were German, sometimes Hungarian, and each had their own way of spelling the names in the record. A further complication was that some ministers decided that the records should be in Latin, and they used, or created, Latin versions of the names. So, over a period of more than 160 years from the 1730s, the church records alternate between German, Hungarian, and Latin. Hence it is very likely that some of the inhabitants had their surnames varied or changed without even knowing. Christian names are not much help in tracing, since parents lacked imagination in naming their offspring. Often the first son would have the same name as his father, and the daughter that of the mother. It was not uncommon for there to be three "Franz" and three "Elizabeth" in successive generations, along with uncles, aunts and cousins all with the same Christian and surnames.

Elek's "Golden Age" was the second half of the nineteenth century. Animal rearing had always been profitable, but its growth was restricted by the need to drive the animals to the more populated areas and cities in the north of the country. With the building of the railway from Budapest to Arad, completed in 1858, and which passed within six kilometres of the village, the markets became easier to reach. The completion of a spur of the railway to Elek in 1881 provided even greater incentive for growth. The industry expanded rapidly, and pig-rearing became predominant. The area of the plain around Elek became the major pig-producing area in Hungary, indeed for the whole of the Habsburg Empire, pigs being sent as far as Vienna, Dresden, Leipzig and Prague. The fertile soil was excellent for growing corn to feed the pigs. Many cows were kept as much for their dung as for milk in order to maintain the land's fertility. The farmers formed co-operatives, which enabled them to buy the best and latest farming equipment. They became the most efficient pig producers in Europe at the time. At the end of the nineteenth century many of the richest people and biggest taxpayers in the whole region were Elekers.

The trade declined considerably after a bad epidemic of swine fever in 1896, and never recovered its dominance. During the First World War seventy-five per cent of the corn grown to feed the pigs was confiscated by order of the Hungarian government, and this effectively killed off the trade.

By the 1860s, the power of the Habsburg Empire had shifted from Austria to Prussia. The Hungarians, who believed they had always suffered discrimination under

Austrian control, were able to demand and get autonomy within their own country. The Prussians were not interested in supporting German-speaking settlers in Hungary, and the Austrians no longer had the power to do so. The Hungarians removed Germans from any high official positions they held. Hungarian was made the only official recognised language, but churches were allowed to decide the language used in their own schools, and some communities obtained special permission to use other languages.

In 1910 the population of Hungary was around twenty-one million. Ten million of these were Hungarian-speaking Magyars. There were over two million German-speaking descendants of the original settlers. The remaining nine million were mainly Rumanians, Serbs and Croats. In parliament the Magyars had over 400 representatives, the remainder of the population eight. The southern Germans had none. The Germans were not happy with their situation, to the extent that between 1899 and 1911 over 197,000 Germans from the south emigrated, mostly to the USA. There were constant demands by the ethnic minorities for some autonomy, but the Hungarians refused to grant any.

Following the end of the First World War it was decided by the Trianon Treaty that Hungary would be forced to give up two-thirds of its territory. This went mostly to Rumania in the east, and to the creation of Czechoslovakia in the north, and Jugoslavia in the south. Hungary lost many of its ethnic Rumanians, Croats and Serbs to other countries. The southern German communities were split mostly between three countries. 650,000 remained within the newly defined Hungary;

550,000 became inhabitants of Jugoslavia; and 350,000 became Rumanians.

The Hungarian authorities changed their attitude to the remaining Germans, realising that they needed their support, and between the two World Wars they allowed German speech, schools and religion in areas dominated by German populations. Germans also regained positions of power, particularly in the army. By 1930 the German population was 479,000, representing about 5.5 per cent of the total population of Hungary. Of these about 138,000 could speak only German.

Franz was born into the farming community of Elek in December 1930. The Sellner family was one of the better-off ones, because they owned land. There are records, which show that one of Josef's forebears in the middle of the nineteenth century had a major share in a flourmill in the village. It is possible that by selling that business the family were able to buy a small farm and some land. They didn't have to work as agricultural labourers for other farmers, or lease land from one of the big landowners, like most of the local population.

Josef's father had been an alcoholic. Josef was born in 1901. His father died in the First World War, his mother in 1928, and he inherited a share of their land. It wasn't large enough to rent out, so Josef worked the farm himself. He was a tall man, strong, and with large hands.

Franz's mother, Eva, came from a much better-off family. She was born in 1909, so was somewhat younger than Josef. She was small and wiry, with pale white skin and chestnut brown hair. She worked hard, and never seemed to laugh much. She was the sort of person who you know instinctively to be tough, and not one to argue with. She always seemed cold and unfriendly.

Her family was staunchly Catholic. Eva never knew her grandfather, György, who died before she was born. He was born in 1820, married four times, and over the period from 1841 to 1894 had twenty-seven children. Through all his married life he lived in the same house, number 100, Elek. The houses in the village were all numbered consecutively, since this was a new settlement, built to a plan.

Medical and sanitary conditions were poor, and many of the children born in earlier times did not survive childhood. Women often died in childbirth, or from complications. When this happened the men usually re-married, often fairly soon after the wife's death. They had to work to survive, and if there were young children to look after they needed to find a new wife as soon as possible. It is not known how many of the later-born children survived into adulthood, but it is fairly certain that the survivors numbered less than half of the twenty-seven born to György and his four wives.

When György had died, his last wife, Annamaria, inherited the house, but when she died in 1905 there were children, and grandchildren, from all four marriages to claim a share of the inheritance. Eva's father, Karl, born to György's fourth wife, was by then an officer in the army, but he was forced to return to Elek to settle the squabbling amongst the family.

The wealth of Eva's family did not arise from the Berger inheritance. It came from Karl Berger's marriage to Maria Hammer. On the death of her parents she was the sole inheritor of all their property and land, including a farm near the centre of Elek, and good quality farmland to the north-east and east of Elek. Her family traded cattle and horses, and lived off the rent from land leased out to farmers. Karl took over the running of Maria's inheritance. He was very good at it, and Franz always admired his grandfather's business skills.

Hungarian laws of succession stated that, on the death of the parents, all the property should be divided amongst the surviving children. This caused horrendous problems and endless arguments, particularly for farmers. Many farms were sub-divided into smaller units, resulting in poor production efficiency, and constant family disputes. It was not unknown for brothers and sisters to go to law against each other to try to resolve their perceived injustices. Often marriages were "arranged" by parents, so that adjacent pieces of land could be joined together into bigger farms, if the neighbouring offspring were of the appropriate sexes and of marriageable age.

This was how Franz's parents came to be married. Love had nothing to do with it. Certainly they would not have married by choice. Eva had been seeing a teacher whom she hoped to marry, but her father intervened. Although he was not keen on Josef's family, being aware of their history of alcoholism and instances of mental instability, the logic of joining together Josef's land with adjacent land of his own was inescapable. Eva had a brother, Anton, and their father did not intend to leave similar problems to be resolved to those he'd had to sort out on the death of his own father. Eva believed she had been allocated the poorer share of her father's property compared to her brother. She did not want to marry Josef, but she had little choice. The marriage settlement enlarged the farm to a workable unit, capable of providing a living for a family. They were married in the autumn of 1929, but from that time until the impending invasion by the Russians in 1944 Eva refused to speak to her father, not because she had been forced to marry Josef, but because she thought she should have been given more land.

When she finally did break the silence her father said to her, "I don't know why you are making such a fuss. Anton, your brother doesn't have any children, so your family will inherit everything when he dies."

So in 1929 the two families' land was joined together to form one farm, though this was quite small. They grew corn, and kept a few cows, pigs, chickens and geese. They also had a few fruit trees. Once a week Eva would take some produce to the market in Elek to sell. This enabled them to buy flour, and, together with their own produce, they were largely self-sufficient. Eva's father tried to help on one occasion by giving them a horse to pull the cart to market. Unfortunately the horse had other ideas, and didn't want to pull a cart. Instead of returning the horse to her father Eva decided to sell it and keep the money. Her father was not pleased, to say the least.

Life was hard. Both Josef and Eva worked seven days a week, dawn till dusk on the farm. A proportion of harvested crops had to be carefully stored in order to provide food for the family and the animals through the bitter winters. Plums and apricots were bottled so that they would have some fruit to eat during the times when there was no fresh food available. There was little entertainment.

Farmers and their wives would often congregate at one of their farmhouses for an evening. The men would talk, smoke, and drink wine or beer. The women preferred to embroider as they chatted, and many intricate patterns were handed down in families from one generation to the next.

Franz was born in 1930. His birth had been a very difficult delivery, and his mother had barely survived the ordeal. The doctor had warned her that further pregnancies could prove fatal. And so sex between Josef and Eva was banned. Franz was therefore an only child, something of a rarity in the predominately Catholic area. Josef took to visiting the whorehouse in Elek, but Eva could tell when he had been there, shouting and hitting him on his return. Being a good Catholic she always forgave him, and there was never any question of divorce. She had not wanted the marriage, but once she had gone through the ceremony in church her faith told her that they would always be married in the eyes of God, no matter what happened in the future.

They had a reasonable sized farm, and as Franz was an only child, he would inherit everything on his parents' deaths. His childhood was hard, filled with work. His mother was not by nature affectionate, and his father needed little excuse to beat him. Franz knew, though, that his future was reasonably assured. Josef could not see any point in Franz bothering with much formal education, apart from being able to read and write. When he had homework to do Franz had to hide so that his father didn't see him doing it. The boy was quite bright and would have liked to further his education. His mother wanted this too, but his father wouldn't hear of it. His father made him work long and hard on the farm, even when he was very young. His future would certainly be on the farm.

The reality proved to be very different. Josef, in common with many Hungarians, failed to understand the harsh lessons of the World War, which had ended just a few years earlier, with its devastating effect on the country of Hungary. What had happened before might happen again in the unstable politics of the 1930s in Central Europe.

# Chapter Two

HUNGARY HAD, QUITE naturally because of its position as part of the German Empire, fought on the German side in the First World War. It did not escape the harsh reparations enforced by the victors of that conflict. In 1914, before the war started, Hungary had occupied an area of 282,000 square kilometres, including large parts of Rumania, Serbia, Croatia and Slovenia. Its southern border with Serbia was the Danube, and Belgrade was a border city on the south bank of the river. When the Trianon Treaty was signed in June 1920 Hungary was left with 93,000 square kilometres, less than a third of its former territories. Large chunks of land were given to what was to become Jugoslavia in the south, Rumania in the east and south-east, and to the creation of Czechoslovakia in the north. Three million Hungarians, including many ethnic Germans, found themselves living in different states, whether they liked it or not. Even following these boundary changes there remained other ethnic minorities in Hungary, mainly Slovaks in the north, and Rumanians in the south-east. As in Germany, the harshness of the reparations following the First World War were to be a major factor in bringing about Hungarian involvement in the Second.

It had taken several boundary commissions after 1918 to fix the new boundaries in the south and east, and these changed more than once, because there were few natural boundary lines across the Hungarian plain. From north of Budapest the Danube runs due south through the middle of the country before turning east on its long journey to the Black Sea. Up to the end of the First World War the south-eastern arm of the river formed a natural boundary with Serbia, as established by Prince Eugen and the Habsburg armies in the 1790s, and the Carpathian mountains the boundary with Rumania. After the First World War Serbia and Rumania were greedy to acquire territory from the defeated Hungarians, and the major powers wanted to make sure that Hungary's power position in the centre of Eastern Europe was destroyed forever.

So it was that the village of Elek, which up to 1918 had been situated in the middle of the great plain of Hungary, found itself in Rumania from April 1919. The population, being mostly of German and Hungarian origin, was not happy with this situation at all. The border commission was organised by French occupying forces in the large town of Arad, a few miles to the south of Elek. The Elekers organised a special train and 400 of them went to Arad to protest to the commission. Luckily the tailor in Elek could speak fluent French, and he acted as spokesman. This protest had the desired effect with the result that Elek, with its 8,000 or so inhabitants, once again became a Hungarian village on 4th June 1920.

This did not resolve all the problems. Many Elekers had relatives who now lived over the new border in Rumania. Large areas of meadowland, which they had used for fattening cattle, were now in Rumania, although a small area of this land was returned to Hungary in 1923. Over a period the rest of this land, which could not be accessed by the Elekers, was sold to Rumanians for a fraction of what it was worth.

Crossing the border was deliberately made difficult by the Rumanians. Over the years the Elekers lost contact with their relatives over the border. The First World War changed the life of the area forever. From being a thriving farming community in the middle of the Hungarian Plain Elek became a sleepy village 500 metres from the Rumanian border. It still had excellent farming land, but its use was changed from mainly animal rearing to growing cash crops of sugar beet and hemp.

To Hungarians the loss of so much territory after the First World War was grossly unfair. Even so, the rise of Fascism in the 1930s wasn't greatly supported in Hungary. The country had had a series of governments following the end of the First World War, but the old systems hadn't changed greatly. Much of the land was still owned by the same families of nobles who had held it since the eighteenth century, despite attempts at land reform. These families also provided the ruling parties in the Hungarian parliament. Many of the Hungarian army officers were of German descent.

After the First World War Admiral Horthy had been installed as Regent, and he had extensive powers that enabled him to change governments and prime ministers.

Hungary regained a measure of prosperity in the years following World War I, and if it hadn't been for its historical links with Germany and the anger of the population regarding the loss of so much territory, it might never have taken the German side in the Second World War. Most of its rulers and inhabitants were no lovers of the Nazis, but they wanted the return of the lands lost. The rulers represented older values of the right, which derived from inherited wealth from land possessed and handed down through generations. Many regarded the Nazis as vulgar.

The influence of Germany grew when Hitler acted against Czechoslovakia, as a result of which Southern Slovakia and Carpatho-Ukraine were given back to Hungary in November 1938.

Pro-German ministers were brought into the Hungarian government. Under pressure from the far right-wing Arrow Cross Party, which was predominately made up of German speakers and Nazi sympathisers, two major laws were passed in 1938 and 1939 to reduce Jewish influence. The second of these laws effectively banned all Jews from employment in the public sector, and severely restricted their operating in the private sector. There was, however, sufficient opposition in parliament to restrain the use of physical persecution against the Jews. Anti-Semitism was prevalent in most of Europe at that time, and in Hungary it was reinforced by Nazi pressure following Hitler's return of land to the nation.

Ethnic Germans were allowed to set up folk organisations, which were really fronts for the establishment of Nazi influence and indoctrination. Many of the young, who were native German speakers, were encouraged to join these organisations. Some even went to "Youth Camps" in Germany, where large-scale indoctrination into Nazi ideology took place.

There was a backlash by the majority native Hungarian nobles in parliament, who felt that the German-speaking minority had been given too much power, and the pro-German prime minister was removed. His successor was Count Teleki, who tried to keep Hungary independent of Germany. After Germany over-ran Poland in September 1939, Teleki allowed 130,000 Polish soldiers to enter Hungary as refugees. He refused to allow German soldiers free movement through Hungary. Under pressure from the Arrow Cross party anti-Jewish laws were brought in, but not harshly enforced because Teleki's government fought to prevent such persecution.

In order to try to gain popular support in Hungary Hitler ordered Rumania to return part of Transylvania and the Nordsiebenburgen region back to Hungary in August 1940. He expected the Hungarians to respond by giving Germany total support in the war. Following this and under great pressure from Hitler and right-wing factions within the country, Hungary joined the war on the German side in November 1940.

Teleki tried hard to keep Hungary out of the fighting, but under pressure from Hitler to allow German troops into Hungary, Admiral Horthy finally over-ruled him at the beginning of April 1941. As a result of this decision Count Teleki committed suicide on 3rd April 1941.

Following this the Hungarian army joined with the Germans to attack Yugoslavia. The Germans were determined to control the invasion, so the force consisted of Hungarian Germans, mostly Danube Swabians from the south, under the command of German Nazi officers. In June 1941, Rumania attacked Russia and after a few days Hungary sent 45,000 troops to aid the attack. The Hungarian force suffered huge casualties and the troops were withdrawn at the end of 1941.

Josef had done compulsory military service in the 1920s, and he was called up to join the force. In the first offensive on the Russian front he was shot in the foot and sent home.

The majority of the Hungarian population had no real wish to take part in the war, but the country had gained return of land as a result of Hitler's power, and they felt they had to support the Nazi cause. Even so the government in Hungary tried to keep the country's involvement as small as possible. Germany received large supplies of food from Hungary, although from 1942 onwards the Hungarians did not receive any payment for these supplies. At first, Hungary provided little in the way of military support. Hitler could not allow this situation to continue, and following tremendous political pressure and open threats by Germany to invade, Hungary committed almost its whole army of 200,000 troops to the Eastern front late in 1942. On 12th January 1943 the Russians attacked the Hungarian section of the front. 50,000 Hungarian soldiers were killed or froze to death. 70,000 were taken prisoner or disappeared. The army, consisting largely of poorly equipped and trained conscripts and reservists, was smashed and fled.

A new prime minister called Kallay was appointed in Hungary. He was pro-British, and secretly prepared to withdraw Hungary from the war. During this period there were no restrictions in Hungary on listening to foreign radio. The neutral press was freely available in Budapest. The government banned discussion of Nazi ideology, forbade media statements saying that Germany would win the war, and allowed a few left-wing delegates in parliament.

After the surrender of Italy in September 1943, Britain approached Hungary through secret diplomatic channels and demanded surrender. Britain and its allies knew that Hungary had never been totally committed on the German side, nor had allied planes crossing the country been fired at, and there had not been any organised allied bombing of Hungary during the war. They were hoping that surrender by Hungary would prevent the westward spread of Communism in Central Europe when the war was over. German spies learnt of these secret negotiations, and on 19th March 1944 German troops arrived in force to occupy Hungary without facing much resistance. A pro-German government was installed. All men and boys considered to be of fighting age were conscripted into either the German or the Hungarian armies, under German control. There was mass internment of anti-German politicians, opposition leaders and those on the left.

The anti-Jewish laws were strengthened and rigorously enforced. In the space of three months from May to July 1944 600,000 Jews were sent north out of Hungary by train to extermination camps. Some managed to hide in Budapest with the help of Hungarian sympathisers, and some did return after the end of the war, but over 560,000 Hungarian Jews died in that short period at the hands of the Fascists.

At the end of September Admiral Horthy, who was still regent, sent emissaries to Moscow to try to negotiate an armistice. On 15th October 1944 he proclaimed Hungary's withdrawal from the war. On the same day German paratroopers arrested Horthy, his family and advisors, and they were imprisoned. The extreme right Arrow Cross party took control with Szalasi as leader. There followed a five-month reign of terror, during which thugs taking instructions from Szalasi roamed city streets, particularly in Budapest, seeking out and killing any Jews, left-wing sympathisers, or opponents to Arrow Cross.

By 26th December 1944 the Russian Army had surrounded Budapest. German resistance was fierce, and there was a siege, which lasted for six weeks. Over the period since March 1944 the Germans had plundered out of Hungary everything they could move. Somehow they managed to remove animals, food, art, gold, machines and even sections of factories. Large numbers of ethnic German civilians fled with the retreating German army, but these were mainly from the cities and larger towns.

For most of the war the rural areas had remained fairly peaceful. Of course, many of the young men had joined the army, and many were lost in action or froze to death on the Russian front. But farming carried on. The old land-owning magnates suffered most financially, because they controlled the large estates, and their produce was taken away by force if necessary, often without payment. There were rigid price controls and high taxes in any case, so many of them were ruined. Many of the small farmers were able to survive by supplying the black market, and by bartering locally.

On 20th December 1944, Russian officers with 350 soldiers arrived in Elek. They demanded a full census of the population, giving as the reason that the information was needed for the issue of ration books. This was untrue, but it achieved an accurate result.

Once in possession of this information the Russians put up lists of names requiring most of the men of German descent between the ages of sixteen and forty-eight, and women between the ages of seventeen and thirty-five to report to the Kulturhaus on 1st January 1945. Many of those in these age groups were married couples, often with young children. The Russians made no orders concerning the children, other than that they weren't to report with their parents. So parents in that situation had no alternative but to find someone to look after their children. Grandparents or family friends were forced to take the children. Those on the lists were to bring enough food and clothing for three weeks, and were told that they were needed to go to work to re-start the factories in Hungary.

Josef Sellner's name was on the list. Eva's wasn't, because she was over the age limit for women at the time. Eva's brother and sister-in-law, Anton and Terezia, were both on the list, and forced to go.

Josef packed some clothes, and Eva packed as much food as he could carry. He put on his thickest coat against the bitterly cold temperatures, and Eva and Franz walked with him along the frozen track the three miles to the village centre. He joined the mass of people outside the Kulturhaus, where eventually he was marked present against his name on the list, and was made to go inside. Eva and Franz made the long journey on foot back to the farm.

Now Franz would have to work even harder on the farm.

A total of 1,100 people were assembled in the Kulturhaus, and forcibly detained there for ten days.

A number of those detained were conscripted to adapt forty rail wagons. Wood-burning stoves were taken from local houses and set up in the wagons. Small beds were made from rough planks of wood, and holes made in the floors of the wagons for toilets. It soon became obvious to Josef and the rest of them that the journey was going to be further than anywhere within the boundaries of Hungary.

On 8th January those in detention were told the truth, that they were to be sent to Russia as forced labour.

At 5 p.m. on 11th January 1945, the first train set off. The wagon doors were locked to prevent any escape. Travel was very slow due to war devastation of the railway, and lack of fuel for the engines, which kept breaking down. It was the middle of winter and some nights the temperature dropped to minus forty degrees. The passengers were tightly packed in total darkness, apart from what light there was from the fires in the stoves, but the combined heat of so many tightly packed bodies helped to stop them from freezing to death. There was no segregation of men and women, and no privacy when the toilet was needed, but few of them were concerned about that.

It took until 2nd February for the first train to arrive in the Ukraine. It must have looked strange for the locals watching the unloading of these trains to see these still reasonably dressed people clutching their luggage being herded by the guards. Certainly those arriving were in a much better physical state than the local population. That situation changed very quickly.

The arrivals were divided into groups and put into camps. They were put to work, men and women alike, in mines, in the forests, or on building work. A very large number of the local populace had died in the war, both civilians and armed forces. The Germans had been the cause of all the misery, and now had to pay the price. They would provide the manpower needed to try to re-build the smashed homes and devastated infrastructure, even though the latter had never amounted to much in most of the poverty-stricken rural areas of Russia and its satellites.

Josef found himself in a group of over 100 men and women being driven on foot by guards armed with rifles across bare frozen grassland for over an hour. Light snow was falling as they reached a fenced compound containing four small, badly constructed wooden huts, which appeared to have been recently knocked together. The new arrivals were split into four groups of twenty-five, with no segregation of men and women, although the men outnumbered the women by more than two to one. Josef was pushed with his group into one of the huts. At least they all knew one another, and those who suffered the worst outward signs of distress got some comfort from neighbours and friends.

One of the women, a widow, had been unable to find a home for her young child in Elek. She had hidden the child under her long skirt when she entered the Kulturhaus, but when they arrived in the Ukraine it was impossible to conceal the child any longer. The Russian guards took pity on the child, and looked after both mother and child.

The huts had no windows, no light, and no heat. Sleeping was in bunks with beds thirty-five centimetres wide. They were given one meal, in the evening, which was always the same, a small piece of bread with some soup, which was mostly water. Some still had some of the food they had brought with them, but that soon ran out. After that the only meat they got was if they were lucky enough to catch and cook a rat.

The guards took any clothes and shoes they fancied. Many of the workers had brought their bibles with them, but the guards stole these and used the paper to make cigarettes. Anyone who protested was put in jail, which was a cellar. Josef spent a lot of his time there. It was very dark and cold, with no furniture of any kind. It was worse when the spring thaw came because it was flooded to a depth of up to thirty centimetres, which made sitting or lying down almost impossible.

Each day they were marched to work, which, as long as the ground remained frozen, was in a forest more than five kilometres away from the camp, where they felled and moved timber. The working day lasted as long as it was possible to see in daylight. The working week was ten days, followed by one day's rest. But Spring was on its way, and although some of the weaker or sick ones died, many survived that winter and were able to work.

Josef was taken at first with a group into the forest. They were to chop trees for house building. When they had first arrived the ground was frozen to a depth of over a foot, which made digging impossible, but when it thawed they were transferred to the building of wooden houses, meant to replace those destroyed in the war.

But Josef did all he could to avoid doing any work. He frequently found places to hide. The guards searched for him. When they found him he was clubbed for disobeying orders. He was taken back to the camp, where he was put in the jail, and kept without food for days on end. The camp commander ordered Josef to be sent with a different group to work in a coal mine. But still he found ways to avoid work. He was becoming weak and very thin, but no matter what was tried they could not make him work.

Finally the commander came to the conclusion that Josef was mad. He was on the verge of starving to death, but still would not agree to work. His behaviour had become erratic, and sometimes he screamed and shouted for no reason. The commander decided there was no point in trying any further. Josef was taken from his hut and put with over forty other people who were too ill or injured to do any work.

In October 1945 a train arrived in Elek containing forty-five sick and injured men and women. They were the first to return from the Russian camps, and for the first time the remaining inhabitants of Elek learned what had happened to their relatives and friends who had been packed into the trains the previous January. Until then all information allowed into the village had been strictly controlled by the authorities, and false news was often put out, so that the locals were never sure of what was true until the return of these villagers.

Josef was one of them. He was taken to his father-in-law's house in the centre of the village, whilst someone was sent to tell Eva and Franz of his return. All the cattle and horses had been appropriated by the new authorities, so Franz and Eva pushed a small cart along the long track to the village. Franz helped lift his father onto the cart and they took him back to the farm.

He was too weak to take solid food. He was fed milk and soups at first, but it was several months before his physical health returned. Those closest to him said he never did recover his mental health. There had been a history of mental illness in the Sellner family, and it seemed the harshness of the conditions on the train and in the camp had pushed him over the edge.

Yet, compared with those who remained in the camps in Russia, he could be considered to be lucky. They worked on through the autumn and winter of 1945. But most had become weakened by lack of proper food and the punishing work schedule. By now they had only the clothes and shoes they stood in. The clothes were rags, and the shoes fell apart. They wrapped rags round their feet, which became saturated as they struggled through the snow to and from the work sites. On return to the unheated camp huts they took the rags off, and their feet froze. By January 1946 they looked like walking skeletons. Some became sick and were isolated from the rest. Their legs and heads became swollen. Then they got diarrhoea and two or three days later they died. Several people died each week in the winter. The ground was too hard to dig graves, so the bodies from all the camps in the area were piled into a cart and taken to be stacked in piles in one camp. In the spring all the bodies were buried in mass graves.

Apart from those sent back to Elek as unfit for work, about 300 in total, the survivors worked on in Russia through 1946 and into 1947, when the remainder was finally sent home. Eva's brother and sister-in-law never returned, and were presumed to have died in the labour camps.

But this is only part of the overall picture. According to official figures, about 35,000 people of German descent were sent from Hungary to slave labour camps in Russia. Of these about 9,000 died. About 75,000 Germans were sent from Rumania of which 11,000 died, and 40,000 were sent from Jugoslavia, of which 6,400 died.

In addition, camps were set up in Rumania and Jugoslavia. Thousands of ethnic Germans were sent to these camps, and most of them starved or froze to death. In Jugoslavia, which had never fought on the German side in the war, and where there had been many German reprisals against the population following resistance actions during the war, the Danube Swabians who remained in the country after the end of the war received very harsh treatment. The Communist government, under Tito, passed laws that effectively removed all rights and citizenship from the whole population of German descent. This became regarded as an invitation to the militia and police forces to execute the Germans summarily, without any controls, or fear of reprisals. Many thousands of Germans were killed. Although many Germans in Hungary and Rumania were deported to the West in the 1940s, Jugoslavia under Tito actively prevented their leaving. Of an estimated 550,000 people of German descent living in Jugoslavia in 1940 about 165,000 were thought to have died in the war. After the war many were put to forced labour within Jugoslavia. About 100,000 people of German descent died in camps, or just disappeared. Between 1953 and 1960, 55,000 Germans were allowed to leave Jugoslavia to go to Germany. By 1980 there were just 50,000 people left in Jugoslavia of German descent, less than ten per cent of the number in 1940.

The Rumanians were more tolerant of Germans following the Second World War. German-owned property was confiscated, but many Germans were allowed to stay to work as labourers for the new owners. On the farms they were allowed to live in barns.

In a stroke of political brilliance, the Great Allied Leaders, Truman, Churchill, and Stalin decreed at the post-war Potsdam Conference, that fourteen million "Germans" would be expelled from the East. The reasons for these proposed expulsions were never quite clear. Were these Germans regarded as invaders, who had no right to be in the lands they inhabited? The three leaders' apparent lack of understanding of European history was appalling in its arrogance. Many of these "Germans", particularly in the north, had been there for centuries, and no longer spoke German. Those in Hungary, Jugoslavia, and Rumania had originally been invited in order to re-populate areas devastated by the lengthy Ottoman occupation. Many of them had maintained their German language and culture, because they had built complete new communities in uninhabited areas, but they regarded the countries they lived in as their homelands. In most cases they were descendants of settlers who had lived in their adopted countries for 200 years or more, far longer than most of the immigrant population of the USA, though it is doubtful that such a thought would have ever entered the head of President Truman.

In 1948, after perhaps a total of a million Germans had been expelled from the East, and many others had managed to leave of their own volition, it was finally realised that the logistics of the expulsions were of a scale impossible to achieve. The policy was abandoned as unachievable.

The huge death toll of the Second World War had not ended when hostilities were officially halted. The suffering continued for many years afterwards.

# Chapter Three

MARIA HAD ALWAYS enjoyed writing, and she had kept a diary ever since she had been able to put a story into written words. This was her entry, written 24th May 1945, when she was seventeen years old, translated from the original which was in German.

"At the beginning of the month the roses and other flowers had displayed their full splendour. Every bud developed, every shrub and tree was green, in order to show the wonderful creation of the Heavenly Father.

Bright gleaming rays of sunshine shone over all our lands. Yes, I always thought the old saying was true: 'Everything new that comes in May makes the soul fresh and free!'

But the year 1945 was different. Where normally in the month of May we German folk would toil willingly in our houses and on the farms, a people with strange hard hearts had taken over. The Germans in the village had been stealthily and silently surrounded.

The loyal and peaceful members of the community had celebrated Whitsuntide on 20th and 21st May. Their hearts were still full of sorrow knowing the Son of God had left the earth forever.

They returned to their work in the fields on 22nd May. I was there too. The early rays of sunshine had hardly smiled on us when the first shots rang out shattering the morning silence. Nobody thought much about it, just that there were hunters in the woods beyond the fields.

The work carried on. The shots became more frequent and louder. Everyone had been calmly working, but then began to become very agitated and cried out, 'We are surrounded.'

We quickly returned down the hillside to the village, and then realised that the sound of shooting was coming from over the hill in the next village of Nagymányok.

A few of us quickly packed some food, water, and a few basic things together and fled. But most of the villagers stayed in their homes. In the evening, when the moon and stars were already out, the leaders told our people, 'Keep calm. Nobody will come tonight.'

Many, who got up in the night to listen for signs calmed their relatives: 'You can't hear anything.'

But when the moon and stars had gone, and the morning brought bright clouds, the peaceful village was surrounded by soldiers. Before those who were the first to become aware of this could warn the rest, who in their weariness still slept, the first bullets were whistling above our roofs.

The villagers ran around as if they were mad. They wanted to flee. No chance, when on every path and footbridge stood a soldier. No way to get past. They say, 'Get back!'

Now they heard the beat of the drum, and the announcement, 'Everybody must assemble at the sports field at 7 p.m. Everyone who can walk must go.'

At the field they were herded together, and not well treated, because of the many who didn't turn up. They stood in silence for a long time and watched as the soldiers and their leader ate a big meal. Then 135 innocent people were driven by the soldiers in the gathering darkness to be locked in the Lendler Castle. The elderly, children, young people, without exception.

Afterwards every house was searched. There were some who had stayed to hide in their houses. They heard the soldiers cursing as they stormed around the houses searching through every little corner. Sometimes they were very close to the place where someone was hiding. These people thought they would be killed if they found them. But if they found nobody they went on to the next house.

In the night a few of those who had managed to hide crept from the village and looked for the others who had fled the village before it was surrounded.

My mother and I had already gone. We hid in the cold room of a ruined hut in the forest. But during the day almighty God allowed his rays of sunshine to enter and warm the hut. The soldiers searched the whole area. Many Germans were found and taken away.

The protective hand of God spared us. They searched no more, and did not find us or many of the others. The bullets whistled close by us, but God the protector spared us so that not once, neither day nor night, were we disturbed. With our prayers and trust in him we were able to hold out longer. He would not desert us, although we are lost.

'Faithfully we asked for his support,
and in him did firmly place our trust,
we leave everything to him to exercise mercy,
He will never leave us.' "

*Maria Weiss, Kismányok      24th May 1945*

The war in Europe had officially ended on 8th May 1945.

Now it was time to enforce the peace, and for the victorious to exact retribution against all of those they held to be guilty of fighting for or supporting the defeated enemies.

Many thousands of those of German descent had fled Hungary, Rumania and Jugoslavia to the west into Austria as the German armies retreated, but many in the rural areas, where there had often been little or no fighting, stayed. As the news of German atrocities during the war spread, anti-German feeling became widespread. Those of German descent now found themselves hated by the native Hungarians as well as by the invading Rumanian and Russian forces.

The Castle Lendler, referred to in Maria's diary, was formerly the large home of a nobleman, which had been taken over by the Russians, and was now being used to hold Germans until decisions were made as to their fates.

The morning after the Germans from Kismányok had been taken to the castle a Hungarian officer who could speak both German and Russian arrived to act as interpreter.

Each family was questioned separately. They were asked if they had had anyone in the family who had fought in the war, and if so, what had happened to such men, and where were they now. Of course, most families had someone who had fought. Many had been killed or had simply not returned after the war's end. The whereabouts of Maria Weiss's father wasn't known. Some of the locals had retreated into Germany with the German army and decided to stay there. Some were in hiding in the area, but nobody admitted to knowing that.

After the interrogations had finished, by which time it was evening, the people were assembled together. The senior Russian officer, speaking through the interpreter, made his announcement.

"You will not be allowed to return to your homes. Your houses are needed for Hungarians who have lost everything as a result of the war. You must suffer for the support you have given to the enemy. There will be no exceptions."

❦

About 100 hundred miles to the west of Elek in south-west Hungary lies the ancient city of Pécs (pronounced Paych). The city was occupied by the Turks for almost two hundred years. There is still a well-preserved mosque close to the centre, and the church in the main square has obviously been converted from a mosque. To the north of Pécs lies a large area of wooded hills, higher just to the north of the city, intersected by deep valleys. This landscape stretches for some twenty miles northwards, gradually reducing in height until the land reverts to more rolling farmland. Much of the wooded terrain is too hilly to farm apart from at its perimeters. There are a number of coalmines in these hills, but they are fairly small.

The village of Kismányok is situated towards the northern edge of the hills, in a small dead-end valley. The village is surrounded by low hills on three sides. The only road access is at the north-eastern end. On the northern side there is a small hill which divides the village from Nagymányok, a larger village situated on less hilly land.

When German settlers floated in their "Ulm barges" down the Danube early in the eighteenth century, they gradually dispersed at various disembarkation points. In this part of Hungary the land close to and to the east of the Danube was prone to flooding, so it was easy to persuade some of the newcomers to turn west into the slightly higher and drier lands. In the early eighteenth century some of this area was under the ownership of the Count of Mercy. His agents were quite happy to re-direct the immigrants, ignoring the fact that many were Protestants, and officially not invited as settlers. West of the Hungarian town of Bonyhád some arrived in the area of Nagymányok, which already had a small Hungarian population. Others made their way into the next valley of Kismányok, where there had been very little prior settlement. The tax census of 1720 states that there were Germans in Kismányok in 1719. Nagymányok became a village with a mixture of Germans and Hungarians, both Catholics and Protestants. Kismányok became German, where the religion practised was mainly Protestant. The major differences between the two villages were reflected in the language spoken, and the fact that the children in Nagymányok were taught in school in Hungarian, whereas in Kismányok they were taught in German. Thus the children of German origin in Nagymányok became bi-lingual, though they would have spoken German at home. Many of the German settlers, and their descendants who had lived in Kismányok right up to the Second World War for over 200 years, could speak very little Hungarian at all.

The German settlers in Kismányok gradually cleared the woodland from the slopes of the hills, which surrounded the village on three sides. They divided the land into blocks, so that each farmer had a sloping section starting near the village and going up to the edge of the forest. This land was planted with crops of wheat, corn, peppers and other vegetables, and always had a section for fruit trees and a small vineyard. The farms were so productive that the farmers formed a council to look after their interests. They each contributed to employ someone to patrol the cultivated blocks around the village to prevent stealing of the crops by other villagers, or by gypsies who roamed the countryside.

Their houses and yards were in the village, and each had a small pen for keeping a couple of pigs. These were fed on corn and some of the vegetables grown in the fields. This meant that the farmers were to a large extent self-sufficient. Items that they couldn't produce for themselves could be got mostly by the process of barter.

At six-monthly intervals a pig would be killed, and everyone in the family would help in cutting up, and preparing the carcass. Apart from that meat, which was not easily preserved and had to be eaten fairly quickly, most was to be stored in some form or another, to be eaten over the next six months. Some was salted and / or smoked, brawn and sausages were made. Nothing was wasted. Pig-killing time was a few days of very hard work. The farmers understood well the old saying that "the only thing you can't use from a pig is its squeak!"

Kismányok was always a small village. Its geographical restrictions couldn't allow much expansion. There was a lot of inter-marrying amongst the families. The Germans in the area originated mostly from the Hessen region of Germany and were predominately Protestant. All social activities centred around the church. There were festivals where everybody in the village joined in. This was an opportunity for everyone to put on traditional costumes. There were processions and dances in the evenings. Every village had its own festivals.

Not everyone was a farmer or owned land. Some worked as hired hands on the farms.

There was always a steady flow of casual labourers coming to the village to help at harvest time, or at other busy times of the farming year. Liaisons were formed with young men and women of neighbouring villages, particularly during the regular church festivals. Marriage often followed, and this formed the basis for most of the new blood settling in Kismányok.

Maria Weiss was part of a large family. Their earliest traceable ancestor who definitely was born in the village was born in 1802, though it is likely that his parents were also born in the village. Maria's immediate family was very religious. She had aunts and uncles who lived in Vasas, close to Pécs and in the town of Komló in the hills to the south. Another aunt, Anna Moser, lived over the hill in Nagymányok, where Maria had three cousins, Peter, Reiner and Victoria. Maria liked her cousin Reiner, and dreamed that one day they might be married.

Anna and her husband Hans lived in a house owned by the small coal mine, which was dug into the hillside on the Nagymányok side of the hill separating the villages.

Hans Moser had come to Kismányok in 1921, when he was nineteen years old, to work as a labourer on a farm. He was from the village of Szálka, about ten miles to the east of the nearby town of Bonyhád, and not far from the flatter lands of the Danube valley. His family, like most of the German residents of Szálka was Catholic. Hans was born in the village of Belisce, which lies on the Drava River, some miles to the south of Pécs, in June 1902. His father and mother were there, because his father was, at the time, an agricultural day labourer, and had gone to Belisce to work on the harvest. His father Adam had died when Hans was not quite six years old. His mother had re-married, but Hans could not get on with his stepfather. As soon as he was old enough he left home to look for work, and that is how he came to Kismányok. Hans had met Anna Engelhardt at one of the church festivals. They became friends and then lovers. She became pregnant. When the baby arrived there was an accommodation problem, since Hans slept in a barn at the farm where he was working. Anna's parents' house was already overcrowded, but the pair lived there with the new baby boy, Peter.

When they knew Anna was pregnant, the couple had wanted to get married as soon as they could, but Hans needed proof of the details of his birth. This was a problem, because, following the boundary changes of 1920, Belisce was transferred from Hungary to Jugoslavia. The documents arrived eventually, but not before the baby was born. The second problem was that Anna was Protestant, and Hans Catholic. In those times it was rare for either party to agree to change religion. A church wedding was not possible, so the ceremony was a civil one, carried out in Nagymányok. In such circumstances a decision had to be made regarding the religion of any children, so a formal agreement was drawn up and registered that any children of the marriage would be baptised as Protestants.

It was not long before Anna became pregnant again, and a year later, in 1923, a second son, Reiner was born. Conditions at the house became even more cramped, but there was no spare housing in the village at all for a couple with children. As the boys grew the situation became intolerable in the house. Hans decided that they would have to live somewhere else. They didn't want to move far away, because Anna had most of her close relatives in Kismányok and the nearby villages. Hans went to the small coal mine over the hill in Nagymányok to see if there was work available, because he knew that workers in the mine were provided with accommodation.

He was lucky, because he got both a job and housing in a terrace of houses built by the mine for its employees. These were small two-storey houses, but each family lived on one floor. The attic was used for storage, and there was also a small cellar. Hans and Anna were allocated a house near the middle of the terrace. There was basically one large room with a small bedroom to the rear. There was a toilet outside, which was shared by the two families in each house. Unusually for most houses in those days, there was a flushing system, because the mine had constructed a culvert that ran beneath the row of toilets behind the terraces. Periodically the mine would release water to flush all the waste away in one go. Despite this there was no water supply inside the houses. Water had to be carried from a well at the back of the houses in buckets. Hans could get a bath at the end of his shift at the mine, and occasionally other family members could go to the mine to use the baths. Each house had a shared long, narrow garden to the rear, where they could grow vegetables. Each family had a shed in the garden. Flour for making bread was provided by the mine. For a small amount of cash a nearby baker would bake bread in his oven using dough prepared by the women of the houses.

There was one electricity supply to each house, which allowed a light in the centre of the main room. Hans managed to buy a two-way adapter to fit the light socket. In time they were able to run an iron off the socket. They also got an electric stove. The cable wasn't very long, so when the stove was in use it was stood on an upturned bucket on the dining table. They tended to use this in summer, when it was too hot to light the fire for the cooking range. They could have had a plug socket installed by the company owning the mine, but that would have meant their having to pay more rent. They were not supposed to run anything but a light from the overhead socket, so they had to be very careful that the mine inspector wasn't around when they were using the adapter for the stove or the iron. Coal for the fire came from the pit spoil heap, where the miners' wives and children were allowed to collect any lumps left in the spoil.

Hans, Anna and the two boys moved into the house in 1928. Life was not easy for Hans or the others who worked at the mine. The workers alternated on three shifts of eight hours, six days per week, and sometimes they would work Sundays too. As the children grew up they had to learn to keep quiet if their father was on a shift where he needed to sleep during the day. Everyone knew when Hans was asleep, because he snored loudly. Pay at the mine was poor and working conditions were bad. Anna was determined that neither of her sons would work in the mine when they grew up.

Life in this rural area continued as it had for over two hundred years, with little contact with the rest of Hungary, and none at all with the outside world. For many years there was no bus service, and you could make long journeys only by walking to the nearest railway line. The farmers had horses and carts, but the rest of the population walked everywhere. It was little wonder that more isolated villages, such as Kismányok, retained their solid German traditions. There was much inter-marrying amongst the families, and most people in the village were related to each other in some way.

Hans was resourceful, and managed to acquire a bicycle. Sometimes he would use it to visit his mother and other relations in Szálka. Occasionally, when Peter and Reiner were small, he managed to balance the two of them on the bike and take them with him.

A black and white photograph survives, taken by a professional photographer of Hans and Anna together, which must have been taken just before the start of the Second World War, when they would both have been in their late thirties. Even allowing for the sombre clothes they wore, and the formal nature of the pose, when compared with appearances of people of our modern era, at the beginning of the twenty-first century, they looked more than twenty years older than they actually were. The speed at which the people seemed to age was probably the result of their very hard lives.

Hans was not tall, but stocky, and looked strong. His fair hair was short, and by the time of the photo he was already losing it. At that time Anna was thin with dark hair. Despite her harsh life she had a jolly disposition, and it took little to make her laugh. She was always dressed in black. All her skirts and dresses were black, because the tradition was still observed that women who were married or widowed always wore black when in public. Apart from that, Anna did not wear the traditional costume, with an apron over the dress. Back in Kismányok most of the people dressed traditionally, including Anna's mother.

Each of the children was of slim build and above average height. All had fairly prominent high cheekbones, and a distinctive kink in their eyebrows. The high cheekbones were definitely prevalent in Anna's side of the family, together with a distinctive chin, but the eyebrows and somewhat flattened nose of the older boy, Peter, seemed to come from their father's family. It is probable that their mother's family had remained in this region to the north of Pécs for most of the two hundred years since their forebears first came. Their father's origins are less well known, although he was of German descent. Moser was a German name, not too common, apart from in the area of Karlsruhe in modern day Baden Württemburg, from where it was thought his family had emigrated to Hungary in the eighteenth century.

In spite of their poverty, Hans and Anna managed to save a little money. Anna was very industrious and always able to find part-time work, of one kind or another. Then Hans' mother died and he was left some money. With their combined funds they bought a field a quarter of a mile away from the terrace of houses. Though they could not raise all the money, the vendor allowed them to pay off the balance by instalments. They planted the field with corn, peppers, and other vegetables. Then they bought a pig, which they could keep in a pen in the garden and feed with their own corn. None of the other mine families could afford to eat red meat. They kept chickens for their eggs, and as a rare treat would kill a chicken to eat. It was noticeable that Hans' family looked a good deal healthier than their neighbours, who always seemed pale and sickly. Most of these were Hungarians, not of farming stock, but basically labourers with few skills when it came to living off the land. Hans and Anna had been brought up in farming communities, which were used to being almost self-sufficient. The family grew apricots, plums, and tomatoes in the garden. Much of this produce was bottled by Anna to provide a winter supply of fruit and vegetables. Hans fixed racks in the garden shed to hang cuts of pork. The miners had to cut down trees on the hillside to make pit props. Anna collected the wood shavings, and these were burnt in the shed to smoke some of the meat. She was able to make various types of paprika from the peppers.

Nearby in the village there was a lane with rows of mulberry trees along each side. Commercial silk producers knew about this, and approached the miners living in the terrace to get them to keep silk worms. Hans and Anna cleared the attic to keep silk worms fed on the mulberry leaves. They were easy to keep, and produced a steady supply of silk cocoons. Periodically the producer would call to collect the cocoons, for which payment was made by weight—another much needed source of income for the family.

By 1930, some of the culture of the world's new largest industrial power was spreading, even reaching remote parts such as rural Hungary. An enterprising businessman converted a building in Nagymányok to a cinema. It was crude, and at first there were only silent movies, but for the area it was a huge step forward. It was cheap, so most families could afford to go, and children had their own shows on Saturday mornings. Peter and Reiner went regularly. In fact the owner gave Reiner a job. For a few coins in payment, Reiner walked round the streets of Nagymányok with a board on his back advertising the shows.

In October 1933, ten years after the birth of Reiner, their daughter, Victoria, was born. This made the house very crowded. Hans and his two sons slept in the larger room, and Victoria slept with her mother in one bed in the small room.

ও

Peter and Reiner Moser were completely different in temperament and personality.

Peter had no intention of being a farmer or a miner. In fact, he would avoid any form of physical work if he could get away with it. He was a year older than Reiner, but they both attended the same Hungarian school in Nagymányok. They had spoken German at home since birth so they knew only a little Hungarian, and they had to take extra lessons to be able to keep up with the rest of the class. Reiner turned out to be much brighter at school than his brother, and was quick to learn. Peter fell behind and had to be put back a year, the result being that they both ended up in the same class. By the time the boys left school they were both fluent in German and Hungarian.

When Peter left school he started to train as a locksmith,

but didn't like it and soon gave up. He moved to the town of Bonyhád, about ten miles from Nagymányok, where he stayed with relatives and got a job working in a factory. It was whilst living in Bonyhád that he caught tuberculosis and was taken into hospital for several months. The nurses soon learnt that they had to watch out for his wandering hands when they were around him. He grew into a young man very much for the ladies.

When he had recovered he decided he didn't want to work in a factory, and he made his way to Budapest. It was the beginning of 1940. Germany was already at war, but Hungary hadn't yet joined in. Amongst the German communities in Budapest there was a strong Nazi influence, and Peter was encouraged to go to meetings of the German Folk Organisation, which by then was basically a cover for the Nazis to recruit for the German army.

Peter was persuaded to join up, although he was seventeen years old and therefore under age. He wrote to his father, Hans, in Nagymányok, sending him a form of authority to sign, with an ultimatum to the effect that he was going to join up whether Hans signed the form or not. And so Peter enlisted in the German army and was sent for training in Germany.

Once the training was completed, he was sent to an infantry unit on the eastern front. He immediately found himself in battle. His unit was following up a tank advance, when he was shot in the leg. He was taken away from the front and had to spend several weeks in hospital. It was decided that he wasn't going to be able to fight again, and so he was transferred to the medical corps.

For the rest of the war he had a number of postings

in different areas, usually within Germany, although at one point he was in Italy. He was very pleased with this situation. He wasn't involved in the fighting, but had many privileges. At every place he was stationed he soon found himself a girlfriend. By the end of the war he had six girlfriends in different parts of Germany.

He had access to medical drugs and dressings, which became valuable commodities, and he was able to acquire and trade some of these for other items in short supply. He was soon known, amongst the right circles, as a man who could obtain things when others couldn't, for a price.

When the war ended he was captured and put in a prisoner-of-war camp in Germany for a few weeks. There was no point in defeated soldiers being kept as long-term prisoners once the war had ended. After he had been processed through the system, in order to see if he was likely to be wanted for any war crime, which he wasn't, he was released along with thousands of others who found themselves in the same situation. He was lucky to have been captured by the Americans, rather than the Russians.

Reiner was much steadier than Peter. The management at the mine where his father worked learnt of his ability at school. They offered him the opportunity to further his education at their expense, on two provisos. One was that after he had completed training he would return to work for the mine, where he would eventually be given a middle-management position, subject to satisfactory progress. The other was that the family should become "Magyarised", the main point being to change the Moser family name to a Hungarian version. This latter point was the problem. Anna, his mother, had been brought up in the German village of Kismányok, and her spoken Hungarian was very poor. She regarded herself as German. She flatly refused to change the family name, and so Reiner lost that opportunity. That decision was to determine the course of their future lives, though they couldn't have foreseen it at the time.

On leaving school Reiner trained to be a carpenter. Anna was determined that Reiner would not follow Peter into the army, if at all possible. It wasn't compulsory for him to join up at first, and in any case he wasn't eighteen until 1941. Once the young men became eighteen the recruiting officers visited to try to persuade them to join up. Anna always knew when the recruiters were in the area and she managed to hide Reiner until they had gone.

Reiner obtained an apprenticeship in the town of Dombóvár, about twenty miles north-west of Nagymányok, where he was able to lodge with his Aunt Elizabeth, his father's sister, who was married to a Hungarian, Joska Papp. He liked living there with the family and their dog, but his conditions of work were very poor, his employer was a tyrant, and he looked for somewhere else to work. He was able to find a job in the village of Váralja, less than two miles west of Nagymányok. This meant he could live at home. In fact it was close enough for him to walk home for his midday meal in his lunch break. Well, that was the theory. In practice Anna was not good at having the meal ready on time. More often than not Reiner and his father Hans would arrive home to find the meal not ready. That meant that either they found themselves eating "on the hoof" as they walked back to work, or doing without altogether.

Victoria was by ten years the youngest child, so didn't spend much time with her older brothers. She played with the other local children of her own age. Their playground was the tracks and fields in the part of the village near the mine, the long narrow gardens of the houses, and the hillside separating Nagymányok from Kismányok. The fact that the family had meat from their pigs was wasted on Victoria. She remained thin and pale, because she was not a good eater. Often she would eat sugar on a piece of bread, begged from her mother, who never tried to force her to eat the other food available. As she grew she helped her mother with housework and cooking, and with the work in the field tending the crops.

There were always gypsies around the country areas of Hungary. They would call at homes trying to sell firewood, wild mushrooms, or anything they could collect that had a value. They were always in rags. Anna, being a very open and trusting person, would usually buy something from them. These people lived from hand to mouth, and were often desperate. On one occasion they had thrown seed down for the chickens kept by the miners' wives. The seed contained poison. The chickens died, and the gypsies came back after dark to steal them.

When German troops occupied Hungary in March 1944, and the Arrow Cross Party was put in charge, the shipment of Jews to the extermination camps in Germany began. The manager of the mine in Nagymányok was Jewish, though he had married a Christian, and they had a daughter who was about Victoria's age. Victoria, then ten years old, played with the daughter sometimes. Occasionally she was allowed into the girl's room, when she marvelled at her fine choice of clothes. She couldn't get over the fact that the girl had a lovely white outfit just for playing tennis. A far cry from the few clothes possessed by Victoria and the other children she played with!

In April 1944 the police called on the mine manager, and he and his wife and daughter were taken away. Two days later the wife and daughter were allowed to return home, but the husband was never heard of again.

At this time enlistment was made compulsory, and it was no longer safe to try to hide Reiner. He received two letters at the same time ordering his conscription, one from the German Army and the other from the Hungarians. He asked the Hungarian authorities what he should do. They told him that since he was of German descent he could choose to join the German or Hungarian armies. It was accepted in such circumstances that the individual would usually join the German army, on the grounds that, being of German descent, they would receive better treatment there.

In Reiner's case it didn't make much difference, because by the time he had completed the short basic training the Rumanians and Russians were about to invade Hungary and the war was almost over. He was put in an infantry division and helped to man a field gun trying to stop the advance of the Russian Army in Czechoslovakia.

The gun positions were very dangerous, and casualties were high. Some of the longer serving troops had become hardened, almost oblivious to the constant danger. It was the only way they could cope with their situation. Reiner was new to it all, and terrified during every action. There were lookouts watching for enemy shellfire, and they would try to yell warnings when incoming shells were expected. On hearing a warning the orders were for everyone to throw themselves on the ground and cover their head. Some of the old hands had been in the same situation so many times that they would ignore the warning, and just carry on as normal.

On one such occasion Reiner threw himself to the ground, but the soldier standing next to him remained standing. There was an enormous bang. Reiner could feel that the back of his head and neck were wet. He thought he had been hit, but felt no pain. When he looked up he realised that the soldier who had remained standing next to him had taken the hit, and it was parts of his smashed body that had fallen on Reiner.

The noise from this near miss had shattered Reiner's eardrum, and made him permanently hard of hearing. In his later years he wore a hearing aid.

Soon after this the Russians outmanoeuvred Reiner's unit. They were surrounded, and, luckily for Reiner, the German commander agreed to surrender, rather than order his troops to fight to the death. The surviving soldiers were captured and sent to a prisoner-of-war camp in Czechoslovakia. The camp was controlled by Russian soldiers, and treatment of prisoners-of-war was very different from camps in Germany run by the Americans, where Peter had been imprisoned for a time.

The camp was divided into two, the German soldiers being separated from the Hungarians by a wire fence. There was a reason for this segregation. Once a week a number of German prisoners were sent by train to forced labour camps in Russia. Each week a Russian female doctor visited to inspect the men, and she decided the ones fit enough to be sent on the next train. In contrast, the Hungarians were subject to brief interrogation, and following clearance by the Russians in charge, they were put into groups to be sent back to Hungary in marches once a week. Once in Hungary they could return to their homes.

Reiner was sick with dysentery, and very weak. The doctor came round, accompanied by a Hungarian guard. The doctor indicated to the guard those of the men fit to travel, and those who would remain at the camp. The soldier had to mark the clothing on the back of the prisoner with a "1" for those going, and a "4" for those remaining. For three weeks Reiner had a "4" marked on his uniform. He was glad, because he didn't like the idea of the labour camps at all. He gradually got better, until the doctor decided he was fit to go. The Hungarian marked a "1" on his uniform. Reiner spoke to the man in Hungarian, and told him he didn't want to go. The man was surprised that Reiner could speak fluent Hungarian. A little later he came back.

"You really don't want to go on the train to Russia, do you?"

"No, I don't think I will come back alive if I go there."

The man made the "1" on Reiner's uniform into a "4".

Reiner knew time was running out, and he had to do something fast. He spent a lot of time near the fence dividing the German and Hungarian prisoners. He spoke to the Hungarians through the fence. He felt he had more in common with them than the Germans on his side. A few of them were sympathetic, and suggested he crawled under the fence to the Hungarian side. The fence wasn't very secure, and it would be easy to make a hole in the earth to get through. The trouble was he was dressed in a German soldier's uniform, so he would be easily spotted amongst the Hungarians. He had to get a Hungarian soldier's uniform. The Hungarians collectively gathered pieces of clothing, by begging various parts from a number of soldiers, to be able to provide sufficient for Reiner to pass as a Hungarian soldier. The pieces were passed to him one at a time under the fence. Reiner had to wait for just the right moment to put on his Hungarian uniform quickly, and then crawl through to the other side of the fence.

Once there he felt safe. The camp guards knew the Hungarians were to go back to Hungary, so exact number counts weren't important. They wouldn't have noticed one or two more or less prisoners.

After two weeks Reiner was told that he would be joining the next marching group to go. The straggling column set off with just a few guards for the four days' march to the reception centre just across the Hungarian border. Reiner and a few others didn't like the idea of marching for four days, and they dropped to the back of the column. When the rear guard wasn't looking four of them jumped into the roadside ditch and hid. The column slowly disappeared into the distance. They hadn't been missed. They watched the marching column of men until it was out of sight, and then carried on walking, hoping to get a lift from passing transport. An American truck came along, which stopped. An officer on the truck spoke Hungarian, and asked where they were going. The truck was on its way to the border, so they got their lift. They lay in the bottom of the truck as it passed the column of marchers. They got off the truck just before the border, found an empty barn to sleep in, and rested for three days. Eventually the marching column came along, which they joined at the back, and crossed into Hungary.

After a brief interrogation Reiner was soon allowed to leave and then had to make his way back to Nagymányok. But the situation had become dangerous for those living in Hungary who had fought for the German, rather than the Hungarian, army.

ℭ

At the start of the Second World War Hans Moser had been thirty-seven years old, but he had managed to avoid joining the military. At the beginning it was not compulsory to join up, and after the Germans took over the ruling of Hungary in March 1944, he was forty-one. It was considered more valuable for him to help produce much needed coal from the mine.

Following the end of the war Hans' situation was not so fortunate. At the end of 1944 the Russians and Rumanians had pushed the German and Hungarian armies back and were in control of the area. As usual the Russians undertook their local census in order to produce the lists of labourers to be sent to work in Russia. Hans' name was on the list of those to go. Anna managed to avoid being sent, because at the time she was already forty-four years old, and therefore outside the age range for women.

So Hans Moser was put, together with many other

ethnic Germans from the area, on the train which left for Russia in the middle of January 1945. In their case they had been given very little time to make any preparations before they were forced to leave, and there was not much in the way of food that they were able to take with them. They also were told they were going to work in Hungarian factories, and so they weren't anticipating a long journey. They were all very hungry and cold, as the train made its painfully slow journey through Rumania and into the Ukraine.

At one point, when the train stopped in Rumania, there were local people at the side of the track offering soup from an urn to the prisoners. These people had suffered greatly during the German invasion in 1941. The Germans had destroyed everything as they retreated, setting fire to the people's houses, which had no possible military significance, as they went. The local population had every reason to hate the Germans. Although everyone on the train was starving it was said by some that the soup was poisoned and nobody should eat it.

Most didn't, but Hans was so hungry that he decided to risk it. At least it was warm, and relieved the ache in his stomach for a short time. After the train had moved on he became violently sick, collapsed in great pain and within two hours was dead.

It was several months later that a neighbour from Nagymányok who knew Hans, and had been on the train, returned from Russia sent back as unfit for work. Within hours of his arrival he went to Anna's house to tell her the bad news.

Anna opened the door herself, and as soon as she

recognised the visitor, she said, "You've come to tell me Hans is dead."

It is possible that had Anna agreed to allow the family to be "Magyarised", and their name changed to a Hungarian version, Hans would not have been made to go on the train to Russia. It is also possible that those events, which happened to the family after the end of the war would have been rather different. But that is conjecture, and it is unlikely that the family ever considered that what happened to them might have been different.

## Chapter Four

AFTER HIS RELEASE from the prisoner-of-war camp Peter spent almost three weeks making his way back to Hungary, mainly by hitching rides on trucks. By posing as a Hungarian ex-soldier, he managed to beg enough money to catch the train from Budapest. He had got rid of his uniform, and was in civilian clothes. On the train he met a woman from Nagymányok who knew him. She told him it would be dangerous to be seen back home, because the local Hungarians knew he had been in the German army, and would tell the authorities, who would put him in a concentration camp, or more likely, send him for forced labour. She said that he should hide when they got back to Nagymányok, whilst she would go to tell Anna where he was.

By this time, in mid-May 1945, Anna and her daughter had been forced to leave their home in the upstairs of the terrace in Nagymányok. Following the taking of the area by the Russians and Rumanians at the end of 1944, and the removal of those sent for forced labour in Russia, the new authorities were determined to make the remaining Germans suffer. There were many thousands of homeless

Hungarian people, particularly in the cities. Some of these were to be sent to rural areas, and were to be given houses still occupied by German families.

Since there were fewer German families in Nagymányok, compared with Kismányok, it was the local Hungarian police who had the job of dealing with them, rather than the Russian troops. Two officers came to the door of the terrace house, and told Anna that they had to move out immediately into the ground-floor house. This had two rooms, and was almost identical to their own, but it was still occupied by their neighbours, an older couple of German descent. They were made to move into one of the rooms. Somehow Anna managed to squeeze most of her furniture into one room, and the rest was put into the attic. By that time there was no pig to look after, since all livestock had long ago been confiscated by the authorities.

When Anna was told of Peter's return she went in the night to where he was hiding and took him back to the flat. The German couple would not tell the authorities he was there, despite their enforced reduction in living conditions.

Anna told him, "It's impossible for you to stay in Hungary. They'll come for you, and you will be sent to a labour camp. I don't want you to die like your father did. You have to get out of the country."

"I can't get out. I don't have the right papers to get across the border."

Soon afterwards Reiner arrived by train. On the train he had met a neighbour, who had told him what had happened to his father. Reiner cried. She also told him that it was dangerous for him to be seen in Nagymányok, because the authorities were looking for and arresting all those who had fought for the Germans. Reiner too had to hide when he left the train, until the neighbour had told Anna where he was, and she came to take him to the flat in the middle of the night. So now both Peter and Reiner had to hide in the one room of the flat, never daring to go out until the middle of the night, and then staying close to the house.

They couldn't do much in the confines of the house. Reiner used his carpenter's skills to make a chess set, and he and Peter had lengthy games to help relieve the boredom.

Reiner wanted to get rid of any evidence of having fought for the German army. He spent hours with a rubber eraser, painfully trying to remove the tattoo spelling of his blood group, which had been inserted into his upper left arm when he joined up, as it had with all the other German soldiers.

Peter knew he had to get out of the country. Many others who had fought with the Germans were being taken away and put into camps. Thousands of Germans died in these camps of disease and starvation, though this was more so in camps in Jugoslavia, where few were to survive.

He had a girlfriend in Budapest from before the war, Christina, who he had kept in touch with by letter. She was of Hungarian origin. He knew that she worked in a government office, and he thought that she could get papers for him, which would allow him to get out of Hungary. He wrote a letter to her and asked her to come to see him in Nagymányok, but she was to tell nobody of the visit, or that he was there.

Christina caught the train from Budapest to Bonyhád, and then a bus to Nagymányok. Anna, Reiner and Victoria had never met her before. She had long dark hair and a very pretty face.

It wasn't possible to have a private discussion between her and Peter in the confines of the flat, but neither Peter nor Reiner could risk going outside in the daytime.

And so Peter had to profess his love for Christina in front of the others. She was wary of him and said, "You are only saying this because you need my help. What about all your other girlfriends?"

"There are no others. You are the only one for me."

His young sister, Victoria, could stand no more of this from Peter. She went to the drawer in the cupboard and took out a small pile of photographs, which she placed on the table.

"What about these girls then, Peter?" she said.

Christina grabbed the photos which Peter had had taken of himself and his other girlfriends in various parts of Germany. She looked through them quickly, got up, and stormed out of the house, away back to Budapest.

Peter was very angry with Victoria, but it was too late. There was nothing he could do.

The two brothers continued to hide in the house. Most of the people who lived nearby were Hungarians, and they knew that any returning soldiers were supposed to report to the police, so it was essential that Peter and Reiner didn't show themselves.

But Peter was careless once when he went near to the

outer door. It had a glass panel at the top, and he saw one of the women neighbours looking at him through the glass.

Would she report him or not? He dare not take the chance.

During that evening he packed a few belongings together, said goodbye to the rest of the family, and slipped quietly out of the village. He walked in the dark, avoiding the roads, to Bonyhád. In the early morning he caught the train to Budapest. Here he would be unlikely to be challenged, since he would not be recognised, and he was just one of the crowd.

During the day he wandered the streets. He was shocked to see the widespread destruction, and the poor physical appearance of most of the population. He saw the women queuing for bread, and whatever other basic food there was in the shops, which was very little. On every corner there were men in Hungarian soldiers' uniforms, with a leg, or an arm, or an eye missing, begging the passers-by for a scrap of food, a coin, anything.

At seven in the evening he made his way to where Christina lived, because he thought she would have returned from work by then. He managed to get into the block of flats, climbed the stairs to the third floor, and knocked on the door of her flat.

She was very surprised to see him.

"What on earth are you doing here? It's over for good. Do you understand?"

" Please Christina, those girls meant nothing to me. In the war you do things you wouldn't do in normal times. You think every day could be your last. I only want you."

" It's too late now. What future would I have with you? I am going to marry my boss in four weeks time. Go away."

Peter stood there perplexed. For a moment words failed him.

"Well, please help me to get my papers, for old time's sake, if nothing else."

"It's no good. It's too dangerous for me. I can't help you now. Go away before I call the police."

She slammed the door behind him, and he made his way back down to the street.

He walked back to the city centre and down to the embankment by the side of the Danube. He still had a little of the bread left from home, and he got some water from a tap set up at the side of the road. Then he found a dry, sheltered corner and settled down for the night. There were many other homeless people in the area doing the same, and although the police patrols kept an eye on them at regular intervals, they didn't disturb them.

In the morning he went to the train station. He still had enough Hungarian money to buy the ticket he wanted. He took the train west, which was going to Vienna, though he knew he would not be able to cross the border on the train without papers.

It was late afternoon when the train arrived at Sopron, the last town in Hungary before the border, where he had to get off. He wandered around the town until it was dark, and even managed to buy a loaf of bread.

Once it was dark he started walking south towards the Odenburger hills. It was very late in the evening when he approached the border. He could see a watchtower with its searchlight picking out the border fence. The next watchtower was about two hundred metres distant, and the fence wasn't very strong or secure. The ground was uneven, so that the searchlight didn't pick out every hollow. Luckily it was raining, so visibility wasn't good, even with the searchlight. He crept in stages to a hollow next to the wire. There was no sound. The earth was soft and wet, and it took him about ten minutes, in between the sweeps of the light, to make enough space under the fence wire to crawl under.

He crept away in the darkness into the Austrian hills.

It was October 1945.

⁊

The neighbour had, in fact, told the police that she had seen Peter at the flat. The next morning two policemen, guns at the ready, were hammering on the flat door, and Anna was forced to let them in. Peter had already gone, but Reiner was still there. They took him to the police station for questioning.

Reiner was put into a room, and told to sit in front of a big desk. An older policeman came and sat at the other side of the desk. One of those who had arrested him stood by the door.

Reiner was surprised by the apparently easy-going approach.

"How long have you been back?"

"Just over six weeks."

"Did you come alone?"

"Yes, there was no one else with me."

"Do you know of any other Germans hiding in the village?"

"No, I haven't dared to leave the flat since I got back."

"You have family in Kismányok. They all know you there. It would be very useful to us for someone who can move in the German community without suspicion. We think that there are a number of Germans back from the fighting who are being hidden round here, and in Kismányok. If you can find out for us and inform us where they are, we might be able to offer you some protection."

"What if I refuse?"

"Well, things could become very unpleasant for you. We would have to hand you over to the military authorities, and then—who knows?"

Reiner didn't know what to do.

"You are asking me to turn traitor against my own people. That's a lot to ask. I need to think about it."

"All right. Go home now, but report back here at ten a.m. tomorrow. We want your answer then."

Reiner went home.

After midnight he slipped out of the flat, carrying just a little food and water. He was grateful that it was the Hungarian police who had caught and questioned him. They weren't the most efficient police in the world, and hadn't even put a lookout on the flat. Thankfully there weren't any army patrols. He was able to avoid the checkpoints by using fields and woodland paths where he had played as a child. By dawn he was twelve miles away. He was glad he had kept moving, because the night was cold. He rested in a thick wood all day. He never heard any people approach his hiding place, just the sound of the occasional truck on the main road two hundred metres away. When it was dark again he carried on walking. He was going north-west, and at one-thirty a.m. the next morning he was in the yard outside his Aunt Elizabeth's house in the town of Dombóvár. He knocked quietly on the door several times. At length the door was opened a few inches very cautiously by Elizabeth's husband Joska. He didn't speak, but motioned Reiner inside.

Once they were inside, Joska said, "I guessed it was you, because the dog didn't bark." Reiner realised his previous stay with the family, when he had been apprenticed to the awful employer, hadn't been a complete waste of time.

Joska knew Reiner well. He was family and would not betray him. Dombóvár was a Hungarian town, the only Germans being one or two, who, like Elizabeth, had married Hungarians. There were no special police or security forces in the town. Provided he kept a low profile Reiner would be safe here.

ॐ

Most of the population of Kismányok, which was almost totally of German origin, had to leave their homes. Many left the country altogether, never to return. Some made their way to the larger towns and cities, where there was plenty of work available in the re-building taking place. Others were able to move to relatives in other areas, where there was not such a concentration of Germans, and where the rules were not so strictly observed. Some stayed and lived rough in the fields or in forest huts.

The incoming Hungarians were mostly from Czechoslovakia. Large numbers of ethnic Hungarians had found themselves in surrounding countries in 1920 when two-thirds of Hungary's lands had been taken away. An agreement had been made between the new Hungarian and Czechoslovakian governments that equal numbers of subjects would be allowed to cross into the other country if they wished to do so. Some of the new arrivals had even brought farming equipment with them. They had been told that they were to be given houses and land that were unoccupied, and were shocked to find the Germans being evicted by force for them to take over the properties. In fact some of them told the evicted Germans that they would not have agreed to come if they had been made aware of the true situation. But it was too late now to change anything.

Gradually a new community was established in the villages. Most of the house and landowners were now Hungarian, but the Germans who remained became integrated with them over the years by intermarrying. It was many, many years before the Germans were able to accept that they would never get back what had been taken from them by force.

Maria Weiss lived with her mother in the forest and in ruined huts in the hills above Kismányok for over a year. Her brother had gone to fight for the Germans in the war. He did not return, and they never knew his fate. Her father had made his way back from the fighting by June 1945, and he was sent on one of the trains for forced labour in Russia. Maria and her mother worked in the fields for the Hungarians when they could. It was a struggle, particularly in the sub-zero temperatures in winter, but they survived.

At the far end of the village, there was a small farmhouse. It was the last house at the side of one of the main tracks, which led up into the fields. The family who lived there were a little different from the other Germans in the village.

Although most Germans had retained their Germanic surnames, even though their families had been in Hungary for over two hundred years, there were a number throughout Hungary who had changed their names into a Hungarian language version, or had dropped their German name completely to adopt a Hungarian one. Unfortunately, some had changed their names back to the Germanic version either before or during the war, because it seemed the best option to appear to support the Nazis, whether they really did so or not. These families were regarded as Nazis by the Hungarians, and received harsh treatment after the war.

The family who lived in this house had more left-wing opinions, and had retained their Hungarian name of Nagy. As such, they were not treated harshly by the Hungarians, or by the Russian troops, even though the son, Hartmut, had fought with the German Army in Crete.

When it came to the appropriation of this family's farm, nobody wanted to take it over. The buildings had been allowed to deteriorate and were almost dilapidated. It would require a lot of repair work to make the place fit to live in, by most people's standards. This didn't bother the family, as they were used to it. For this reason, and because of their Hungarian surname, they were allowed to stay in their house. They had a field at the top of the track, which went past the farm, where they grew corn, peppers, and vegetables. A little further to the east they also owned a block of land on the sloping hillside, one of a number of blocks side by side round the head of the valley. Here they grew several varieties of grapes, interspersed with apricot and plum trees. At its bottom end, the track that went up into the fields past the farm had been dug down through a low hill to make it less steep, therefore making it easier to transport crops from the hillside above down into the village. One of Hartmut's ancestors had dug a cave into the side of the hill, and put a door to it. The cave had almost the same temperature year round, and was ideal for the fermenting and storage of wine. The family was very lucky in being allowed to keep all of this.

Hartmut, the only son of the family, did not return from the war until the beginning of July 1945. Even though he had fought with the Germans his Hungarian surname enabled him to return home without problems. He was shocked to see that Kismányok had been taken over by Hungarian strangers. Many of his former friends and neighbours had left the village. Others were living rough in the fields, or in the small farmers' huts on the hillsides above the village. He was even more surprised to find that his father, mother, and younger sister would be allowed to stay in their home and keep their land.

Hartmut was one of the few who could return to his life as it had been before the war, helping his father to farm, once the latter had returned from the Russian labour camps. The family helped other Germans who were living rough in the fields as much as they could, by giving them food and shelter during the worst of the winter weather. Eventually these Germans returned to the village to try and find somewhere to live. Hungarians now occupied most of the houses in Kismányok. Maria and her mother were told they must live with the Nagy family.

Before Hartmut Nagy had joined the German army in the spring of 1943 as a twenty-year-old, he had known Maria Weiss as a young fifteen-year-old girl. When he saw her working in the fields in the autumn of 1945 he could see how much she had changed into a pretty young woman. On occasions she worked for the family tending the crops in their field. She helped that autumn in the bottling of plums and apricots, which provided them with their fruit over the winter period. Once Maria and her mother had moved into the farmhouse it wasn't long before Hartmut and Maria got to know each other well and fell in love.

The following Whitsuntide they were married in the church in Kismányok. Hartmut worked hard to improve the farmhouse. Although the house was in need of repair, it was structurally sound, and looked far worse than it was. He repaired parts of broken wall, and fixed the leaks in the roof. He was able to get some paint for the woodwork, and before long the house looked quite neat.

It had been built in the traditional way. There were three rooms in a line with one outside door to the front at the left-hand end as you looked out from the inside, and the long back wall was blank. That meant that to get to the right-hand end room you had to walk through the middle room. The right-hand and centre rooms were used as bedrooms. The room at the left hand was kitchen and living room, though this was quite small. There was an earth toilet outside at the right-hand end of the yard. Next to it was the pig pen, which was just big enough to take two fully grown pigs. At the top left-hand end of the yard was a wooden shed built on to the house at right angles and split into two. This was used for storing food, where meat and vegetables were prepared for cooking and where the fruit harvest was bottled to provide the family with its winter supply. There were no water, gas or electricity supplies to the house. Water was from a hand pump in the yard. The stove in the kitchen burnt wood carried down from the hills above.

And so Hartmut and Maria lived there as man and wife from May 1946. It wasn't long after that Maria's father returned from the Russian labour camps, and he too moved in. The house was very crowded. Hartmut's father was a very nasty man, a bully. He hated having to live with all these people in one house. He expected everyone else to do all the work. Hartmut stood up to him, so he picked on the easiest outlet for his anger, his wife. Her life was made miserable by his actions.

Anna Moser and her family were less fortunate. Her husband Hans was dead. Peter had managed to get out of Hungary into Austria. Reiner was living with his aunt in Dombóvár.

Anna and her daughter lived with the old couple for a time. The wife became ill, caught pneumonia, and died. In a matter of a few weeks the husband had found a new lover who moved into the room.

After Reiner had disappeared the Hungarian police had called to interrogate Anna and Victoria. Although Anna knew where Reiner had gone, Victoria didn't. The police tried to find him, but couldn't. They were angry with

Anna, but she wouldn't tell them where Reiner had gone. The police decided that they had to punish Anna.

One day, when Anna returned home from work she found Victoria standing at the door to the flat weeping. Whilst Victoria had been at school the police had been and boarded up the door to their room in the flat.

Anna went to the police station.

"Where are we supposed to live?" she asked the sergeant sitting behind the desk.

"We don't care what you do. You'd be better off leaving this place all together," he replied.

"So you will turn me and my young daughter out with nowhere to go?"

"That's your problem. You are German and you don't have any rights."

Anna didn't take this very well. She was on the verge of a nervous breakdown, but she was responsible for Victoria and had to find a solution. She had worked occasionally for a butcher in the village of Szárász, about five miles north west of Nagymányok. She took Victoria with her to ask him for help. The butcher said that they could stay at his house, but he couldn't take the two of them for more than just a few days. There just wasn't enough space. He was prepared to give Anna a job, but couldn't take Victoria.

Anna didn't want Victoria to join Maria Weiss and her mother, who were still living rough in the hills above Kismányok. Apart from Maria, the nearest relatives were in Vasas, on the outskirts of Pécs. Anna's youngest sister, Eva, lived there with her Hungarian husband, Mihaly.

The next day Anna and Victoria made the very long

walk to Vasas, which took them from early morning until late evening. They had only the clothes they were wearing. Eva Najadon opened the door and hugged her sister and Victoria.

Anna explained what had happened.

"We will find room for Victoria. She can stay with us until things improve. You can take some of my clothes, Anna. They should just about fit you."

There was no prospect of Anna finding a home for her and Victoria in the near future.

After a few weeks Anna asked Eva for more help.

"What's left of our furniture is still in the attic in Nagymányok. Can we take the horse and cart to bring it back here? It will fit into your shed."

So Anna, Victoria, Eva and her husband made the long slow journey with the horse and cart from Vasas to Nagymányok.

They ripped down the wooden planks sealing the door to the attic. Once inside they got a shock. The furniture was crawling with insects, and covered in mildew. Most of it was beyond saving. They heaved it outside the flat and burnt it.

And so the four remaining members of Anna's family became separated. Hans, her husband was dead, their home and most of their possessions were gone. The future was at best uncertain.

## Chapter Five

JOSEF SELLNER'S HEALTH gradually improved during the winter of 1945-1946. He had to be nursed by his wife, Eva. Franz and Eva managed the farm work between them.

The area of Elek returned to some sort of normality for a time, though major events were taking place elsewhere.

Russian troops occupied Hungary. Stalin was in firm control in Russia, and he intended to install Communist states in all the territories where the Russians were the only occupying force. If, in order to achieve this aim, it was necessary in some of these countries to apply political manipulation, falsify charges against non-Communist politicians, torture and murder opponents, real or imagined, then so be it. The end justified the means.

In Hungary, following an election on 4th November 1945, a new government was set up. The main party in charge was the Smallholders Party, as the name suggests, originally representative of the large number of small landowners. The leadership was weak, and a coalition with other parties was set up to run the country. The Communists, even though they were one of the smaller parties, managed to gain undue influence including control of the most important ministries.

The Communists organised the setting-up of the political police force based on the Russian model. This recruited many of the thugs who had operated for the extreme right Arrow Cross Party during the war. The Party leaders were Hungarians who had spent the war years in Moscow, being trained in Stalinist methods. Over a period of two years, with Russian backing, the Communists under one of these so-called "Muscovites", Rakosi, were able to exploit conflicts between the other parties. Rakosi controlled the Political Police and in January 1947 he had the main leaders of the Smallholders Party arrested as "Enemies of the State". By March, Rakosi and the other "Muscovite" Hungarians effectively ruled the country. The remaining leaders of the Smallholders Party resigned, and new elections were held in August 1947. There was large-scale vote-rigging by the Communists, aided by the occupying Russian troops. The Communists became the biggest party, but even then they had only twenty-two per cent of the vote. Rakosi was able to pass a law banning opposition parties, and Hungary was run virtually by the Political Police under his control, backed by the Russian army and guided by the Russian secret police force.

For the next forty-two years the Communists ruled Hungary. The horrors inflicted by them are not to be catalogued here. They did not directly affect the people in our stories apart from at the very beginning.

The main event that affected the families in our stories occurred soon after the end of the war in July 1945 at the previously mentioned Potsdam Conference. Here it had been decided that ethnic Germans still living in Poland, Czechoslovakia, Rumania, Yugoslavia, Hungary, and other parts of Eastern Europe were to be sent back to Germany. "Sent back" in this context was somewhat strange, since most of these "Germans" were descended from immigrants who had originally arrived in these countries 200 years or more before. No matter, anti-German feeling throughout Europe was running extremely high, particularly as the extent of the Holocaust became more widely known.

How this massive movement of over fourteen million people was to be achieved was another matter—at a time where there was widespread destruction and disruption over large parts of Europe as a result of the conflict. At the end of November 1945 the Allied Commission agreed that the 500,000 Hungarian "Germans" would be sent to the American-occupied zone of Germany, which was mainly in the south of the country. This represented virtually every German remaining in Hungary at the end of the war. In fact, that many expulsions did not take place. From November 1945 to June 1946 about 115,000 Hungarians of German origin were expelled to West Germany. In 1947 about 100,000 people of German descent were sent to East Germany from other parts of Eastern Europe. The remainder, mainly the children and the elderly, were allowed to stay in Hungary, though over the period up to 1950 about another 130,000 Germans made their way out of Hungary to Germany. Not all those expelled remained in Germany. Many were given, and took up, the opportunity to emigrate to America and Canada.

Some areas in Hungary were better at administering these expulsions than others were. In Elek lists were put up at the village hall starting on 10th April 1946. The inhabitants whose names were on the list had to register. They were told when their train was to leave, and were allocated a wagon number. Each person was allowed to take twenty kilograms of food and eighteen kilograms of belongings. They were given, at the most, forty-eight hours' notice.

Josef and Eva Sellner's names were on the lists. Franz went with them to register. They returned to the farm to pack. Franz's grandfather Karl Berger went with them. There was no alternative but to ask him to take the few remaining animals, and Franz helped him drive them along the long track to the village centre. His grandfather and grandmother were being allowed to stay because of their age, but all the land they had owned and leased out had been confiscated and given to Hungarians. They were allowed to keep their farmhouse in the centre of the village, but there was very little land, and most of the animals would have to be sold.

There were six trains in total, which took almost six thousand of Elek's inhabitants of German descent away. Those due to leave on a certain day had to report to the Kulturhaus the previous evening, and they were locked in there until it was time to go. Once the houses were empty some of the remaining Hungarians and Rumanians went in to take any of the possessions they fancied, which the departing Germans were forced to leave behind. The trains arriving brought Rumanian and Slovakian settlers who were allocated the houses left by the Germans. Then the

Germans left on the same trains. Those Germans not being expelled were not allowed to go to the station to say goodbye. Some of the more sympathetic Hungarians and Rumanians did make the effort to go and say goodbye to their former neighbours.

Josef and his family were on the last train to leave on 6th May 1946.

Their grandfather and a friend helped them to carry their bundles along the track to the village for the last time. Nobody said much at all. Eva hugged her father in a way that showed that any physical gesture of feeling on her part was rarely expressed. Josef and Franz shook his hand at the door of the Kulturhaus before they left him to go inside.

The old man walked slowly home with tears welling in his eyes.

In less than three weeks, two-thirds of the population of Elek had been sent away, most never to return to the only home they had ever known. Life in the village in the time immediately following this event must have been very strange, with a new population being installed virtually overnight.

The six trains went to different destinations in southern Germany. There was a shortage of engines, and the trains were often left standing in one place for hours on end. It took each train several days to reach the Austrian border, and ten to twelve days to reach its final destination.

Josef, Eva and Franz were packed into a wagon containing forty people, together with their belongings. It was a relief when the train stopped, and the guards opened each wagon, one by one, to allow the people out to relieve themselves at the side of the track. Then they could get some fresh air. It was early May and quite warm.

Once the train crossed into the American-controlled zone in Austria, everyone had to get off to be disinfected with DDT powder. From there, the train made its slow journey across the mainly rural areas of Austria and southern Germany. Only when it entered a large city did the passengers see the effects of the destruction carried out in the war. At the first stop in Germany a Red Cross carriage with nurses and a doctor was added, so that any sick and injured could receive treatment.

The train carrying Josef and his family went at first to Leonberg, south of Stuttgart, where it was divided into two. The section they were on turned north. The train rumbled through what was left of Stuttgart City centre. The passengers stared at windowless buildings that were just shells. Piles of rubble lay everywhere. People picked their way across the rubble into blocks of flats with no roofs or windows. A few ramshackle trams moving slowly along roads where there were no pavements, just continuous piles of rubble several feet high marking the edge. The only vehicles in decent condition were military cars and trucks. All of these carried the Stars and Stripes. The occupying force in this part of Germany was the American Army.

Josef, Eva and Franz finally left the train at the town of Ludwigsburg, ten miles north of Stuttgart. They were taken to the Baroque Palace in the centre of the town, which was being used as a registration and clearing area. They had to stand or squat on their packages for three hours whilst the queue of refugees was dealt with. When it was their turn, at last, their papers were checked and they were questioned about their background and war record. They were then each given new papers, some vouchers for food and clothing, and allocated temporary accommodation.

Buses were waiting in the yard, and once all those allocated to their particular transport were on board, the bus set off. They were taken to the small town of Kornwestheim, a few miles south of Ludwigsburg. They got off the bus in a compound containing several long wooden sheds. These had been built during the war, originally as soldiers' barracks, but had later been used to house Allied prisoners-of-war.

Males and females were separated into different huts. The huts contained bunks racked in twos, with very little space to move around. For some time they were to experience a little of the life of a POW, though, of course, they were better fed and treated, and they weren't forced to work in the local factories for no pay, as the POWs had been. The huts were constantly full. The authorities struggled to find other places for the inmates to live, so that they could make way for new arrivals.

The family tried to settle into their new environment. One of the first things Eva did was to write to her father back in Hungary to tell him where the family was, and that they had survived the journey without mishap.

Josef was far from well. He hadn't completely recovered physically from his time in Russia, but, worse, he sometimes lapsed into strange behaviour. He imagined things, and was convinced that Eva was plotting to kill him. At other times he appeared normal. The doctors decided that he was not yet fit for work, but that he was likely to recover given time. There was no immediate work for Eva or Franz, who was by then fifteen years old.

As soon as Eva's father received her letter he wrote back. When they had been forced to leave Elek, he had gone to look again at the list containing their names. He had realised that, although Josef and Eva were on the list, Franz wasn't. He was still considered a child, and hadn't been forced to leave. Did Franz want to go back to Hungary? He could live with his grandfather.

The family discussed the situation long and hard. The conditions in the huts weren't good. Nobody seemed to know how long the refugees would have to live there. Franz knew farming, and little else. There were no apprenticeships on offer, and job prospects seemed to be non-existent. It was decided Franz would try to return to Hungary.

Passenger trains were running into Austria, and, as far as they knew, on into Hungary.

They could scrape together enough money from their allowances to pay for the fare.

So Franz made the long journey back to Elek. It was surprisingly easy. He had his new papers, which were good in Germany and Austria, and his Hungarian papers were still valid. He was fluent in German and Hungarian, so language wasn't a problem. Nobody showed much interest in this youth travelling alone, and he was allowed through each of the various checkpoints with little fuss.

Eva had written to tell her father that he was coming, so the old man was not surprised to see Franz standing in the doorway of the farmhouse.

Franz had hoped that he would be able to find work on one of the farms, which used to be owned by his grandfather. Unfortunately, the new Hungarian owners just didn't want to know. They had plenty of Hungarian and Rumanian labour, and there was no reason they should give work to a German, experienced or not. He helped his grandfather with the few animals he was still able to keep at the farmhouse. He walked around Elek, but it wasn't the same. The new arrivals had already made many alterations to the houses. Somehow they didn't look the same any more. Most of his schoolfriends had left. The village was full of strangers, apart from the older Germans, like his grandfather, but he had little in common with them. The age gap was too great.

In addition to this he had not realised, when he had decided to return to Elek, that a law had been passed making it illegal for any Germans who had left Hungary, either by deportation or voluntarily, to return to the country. One of his grandfather's new Hungarian neighbours realised that Franz had been to Germany, and reported him to the police.

He was made to go to the police station, accompanied by his grandfather.

"You were deported to Germany and have come back. Is that right?"

His grandfather took over.

"Yes, but it was a mistake. His name wasn't on the list. He needn't have gone. His mother and father assumed he would have to go because they were on the list."

The officer thought for a moment.

"There is nothing in the law concerning anyone who

leaves by mistake. It seems clear to me. Anyone who leaves Hungary to live in Germany or Austria is not allowed back into this country. He will have to go to Budapest to decide what is to be done with him."

There was no way of changing this ruling.

Franz said to his grandfather, "I don't want to go back to Kornwestheim. Conditions there are bad."

His grandfather gave the matter some thought.

"I have a distant relative who has a farm just over the border in Austria, not far from Vienna. I could write to him to see if he will take you."

Franz agreed. He would like to do farm work again if he could get it.

It took two weeks for the exchange of letters between his grandfather and his relative in Austria. He was prepared to give Franz a home, and some work.

Franz was sent to Budapest by the police before the reply was received from Austria. He was put in the main jail. Conditions were bad. It was damp and he had to sleep on straw on the floor. Such food as the prisoners were given was barely eatable.

A court hearing was arranged for ten days later, at which it was confirmed that he was to be deported again.

Before the transport could be arranged his grandfather was able to get in touch with the court to tell them that he had found somewhere for Franz to go to in Austria. The court wasn't concerned with where he went, so long as it was west to a country not under Russian control or influence.

Franz found himself once again crossing the border into Austria by train, only this time as a fare-paying passenger, rather than a refugee. He got off in Vienna, from where he had to find the bus, which would take him to the village where Klaus, his grandfather's relative, lived. The bus took him to the small village of Jahrndorf, just two miles from the Hungarian border and the same distance from Czechoslovakia, in a low-lying, flat area, to the north-east of the large lake, Neusiedler See. He asked in the village, and was directed to Klaus' farm.

He soon settled into his new home. Klaus was married and had three children, boys of seven and nine, and a two-year-old girl. The farmhouse was quite big, and Franz had a small room of his own. The work was similar to what he was used to; a few cows, pigs and poultry to look after, and small fields of vegetables and corn to tend. Klaus could pay him a very small wage, but his lodgings and food were free, so he didn't need much.

Franz was now seventeen years old. His one expensive vice was smoking. Along with most of his schoolfriends in Hungary he had been smoking since he was fourteen, as much as his meagre funds would allow. Now he was in Austria he was shocked to find that cigarettes cost four times as much as they did in Hungary. The exchange rate was fixed so that one Austrian schilling was equal to one Hungarian forint, but a pack of cigarettes cost ten in Hungary and forty in Austria.

That got him thinking. Here was a way to make some money. The border with Hungary was less than two miles away across the fields. There was no border fence, though Hungarian soldiers made regular patrols, day and night. On the Hungarian side it was only about three miles to the town of Hegyeshalom, where it should not be a problem to buy cigarettes. He had the advantage of being fluent in both countries' languages.

First of all, he decided to try to slip across the border just to buy a few packets of cigarettes for his own use. As soon as it got dark he walked across fields towards the border.

The border in this area was far from clear in any case. The border remained the same as it had been fixed in 1920. Several farmers had their farmhouses in one country, but had been allowed to retain fields, which, if you drew a straight line where the border was supposed to be, had part of the field in the other country. Because of this there was quite a broad strip, which each country regarded as "no man's land".

Franz crossed over without seeing or hearing any patrols, and within an hour he had arrived in Hegyeshalom. Even though it was now after eight p.m. he soon found a shop open which sold cigarettes. He still had Hungarian money and bought ten packets of cigarettes, as much as he thought he could carry in his coat pockets.

He didn't hang around, but set off back towards the border. Once again he was able to cross without a problem, and by quarter past ten he was back in his room. He really enjoyed smoking his first "smuggled" cigarette. He was very pleased with himself. He had discovered his own little business.

So about once every two weeks he made the journey, always in the dark, across the border, returning with cigarettes. By taking his small suitcase he could carry about sixty packets of cigarettes. He made each trip a day or two before he was due to have a few hours off work. Then he would catch the bus to Vienna. There it was easy for him to sell the cigarettes quickly in the streets, for thirty schillings a packet. The streets were full of people of all ages selling a wide variety of products for less than the going rate, or in some cases selling off family possessions just to raise cash to live on. Some of the things sold were valuable, more of it would be classed as junk, but there was nearly always a buyer ready to pick up a bargain. The authorities couldn't control the sales, and turned a blind eye to the practice, unless anyone made what they were doing blatantly obvious.

Franz varied his route across the border, sometimes walking along the banks of the River Leitha, which crossed the border nearby. That way was easier, because there were fewer hedges and fences to cross close to the banks of the river, but he knew it was riskier. He had to be careful to avoid increased numbers of army patrols near the river, which meant more chance of getting caught.

For two months his luck held.

One night he was coming back over the border with his case of cigarettes. This particular route meant his creeping along the long side of a barn, which was almost on the border, and where he had seen patrols before.

It was a very dark, cloudy night. He thought he heard a rustling noise in the grass to his right, so he dropped down onto all fours. Silence: so he carried on, now crawling along the side of the building. Suddenly he felt a bump on his right hip, and there was a soft yell.

"Who's there?" he whispered.

"Who are you?" was the whispered reply.

"Never mind that. I need to get across the border fast."

"Me too, someone might have heard the noise."

They both quickly crawled round the corner of the building and were soon over the border.

Franz was surprised to see that his companion was a young woman. As soon as they felt they were safe they stopped to talk. He could see that the woman was carrying a rucksack.

"Are you bringing cigarettes over?"

"Not cigarettes," she replied, "but things I can sell in Vienna."

Franz said, "It's a bit risky, especially if you bump into other people making the same trip."

They agreed to travel to Vienna together on the following morning, and Franz found a place for the woman to sleep in the barn back at the farm, without disturbing Klaus.

On the bus to Vienna they talked. Her name was Margit, and she was in her mid-twenties. She was a physical education teacher at a school in Vienna, so she was very fit. They agreed to arrange future cross-border trips together. It should be easier for two to watch out for patrols, and they wouldn't bump into each other by accident.

They made three successful trips together, changing the route each time. Margit would never tell Franz what she was smuggling. He guessed it might be penicillin or other drugs and small hospital supplies, but he never did find out for sure.

On the fourth trip, Margit wanted to come back along the riverbank. Franz reluctantly agreed, though he told her he thought it was more dangerous because of the extra patrols near the river. Sure enough, as they were nearing the border, two soldiers with rifles suddenly appeared from behind a hedge and stopped them.

The soldiers demanded to know what they were doing there, and told Franz to open his case. They saw the cigarettes. Margit was talking all the time, saying that it wasn't much, and not worth the trouble to arrest them. One of the soldiers told her to open her rucksack. As she started to do this she suddenly punched the soldier and pushed him hard, so that he fell backwards into the river. There was nothing for it but for Franz to attack the other soldier, or they would both be shot. The soldier was taken by surprise, and he too fell into the river. Margit and Franz turned and ran as fast as they could across the border.

Franz continued to make the trips across the border, sometimes alone, and sometimes with Margit. The trouble was he was becoming a little too cocky as a result of his success, and started to take less care. One night he was stopped by a patrol, and taken to the military officer in charge in Hegyeshalom. The officer saw that Franz was quite young, so he just warned him not to do it again, and let him go. Soldiers took him to a cross-border post, where he was handed over to Austrian soldiers. They checked his papers, and told him to go home.

For the next month he didn't go near the border. Then he started thinking. He had made over a dozen trips across the border. He had been stopped twice and caught once, and only had a telling off. He decided that it was worth the risk.

So he carried out more smuggling expeditions. He hadn't heard from Margit for three months and didn't know where she was. On the third occasion he was caught once again, and taken to Hegyeshalom. He found himself in front of the same officer as on the previous occasion.

The officer looked sternly at him.

"You don't seem to listen to warnings. You have one more chance. If you are caught again you will go to jail."

This time the Austrian border soldiers were stricter too. They took Franz home and told Klaus that he must keep more control over Franz.

Klaus had realised what Franz had been up to, and had spoken to him before about the risks he had been taking. Now he took a much stronger line.

"Look, what you do in your own time is your business, but when I get visited by soldiers it becomes my business. I have given you a home and a job. Don't abuse my hospitality. If there is any more trouble you will have to go."

It was now August 1948. At the beginning of December Franz would be eighteen.

Call it foolishness, or the bravado of youth; maybe it was his usual inability to take on board good advice. Whatever it was, Franz was going to continue with his smuggling operation.

It had been two months since he had been caught for the second time. He would just have to be more careful. What he didn't know was that the Hungarian army had adopted a new tactic in an attempt to stop the cross-border traffic. Four-man patrols were sent out, but split into two groups of two. Each patrol followed the same route, but the second pair followed the first at a gap of five minutes.

Franz got to the border and saw two soldiers walking along. He hid until they had gone past, then got up and walked across the field towards the corner of a barn on the Hungarian side. He hadn't reached the barn when he heard the shout from the soldier. He turned to see two soldiers standing less than fifty yards away, both with their rifles pointed at him.

Next morning Franz found himself in front of the officer for the third time.

"That's it. Now you are for it. Tomorrow you will be taken by truck to Budapest. They will decide what to do with you there."

He was taken in a truck with another three prisoners to Budapest, and put into the jail.

Two days later he was brought before the controlling magistrate.

He stood there not knowing what to expect.

The magistrate read the sheet in front of him, and gave Franz a long hard look.

After a good two minutes he said, "You have three charges of crossing the border illegally, and two charges of smuggling against you. Have you anything to say?"

Franz could say very little, only that he had been desperate for money, which wasn't true.

"Well, the normal sentence for these offences is twelve months in jail. However, I can see that you are young, and Hungary needs recruits for the army. I will give you a choice. Either you go to jail for twelve months or sign up to join the army for two years."

Franz didn't need long to make up his mind. He had already had two brief stays in the Budapest jail, and that was enough.

"I'll join the army."

Training was at a barracks on the outskirts of Budapest. It was very basic, most of the time being spent in drills and getting the recruits physically fit. After three weeks he was regarded as trained, and sent to a camp at Eger, about fifty miles to the north-east of Budapest. The duties of a soldier in Hungary at that time consisted of frequent patrolling of every part of the country. The Communists were in command, but they did not yet feel totally secure. They were determined to maintain a large army presence, intended to display to the population that they were in control, and that no opposition would be tolerated.

Franz hated the life. He just couldn't stand having to take orders. There was very little variety in the daily routine. When on duty there was a lot of standing around doing nothing. The soldiers' activities were restricted when they were not on duty. The army was afraid of soldiers deserting. Most of the time was spent in the barracks. Besides, there was very little entertainment in the small market town of Eger.

One of the other soldiers had a problem at his home. His mother had died, and the army granted him five days' leave to return home for the funeral. The soldier came from Nagycenk, a tiny village to the south of the Neusiedler See, very close to the Austrian border. In such circumstances, the army always sent another soldier as escort, in order to prevent desertion. They chose Franz, because their records showed that he came from Elek, in the far south-east of Hungary on the Rumanian border. In the view of the commander the chance of Franz deserting, or trying to cross into Austria, would be remote.

So Franz found himself staying with the other soldier's

family in Nagycenk. On the day of the funeral he did not go. He wanted to get into Austria, so he made the few civilian clothes he had brought with him into a small package, and set off on foot for a border crossing, less than three miles away.

As he approached the crossing he could see that it was just a small bridge across a river, with vehicle barriers at both ends, and each had a sentry box with a kiosk behind. There seemed to be just two soldiers on duty on each side.

He sat out of direct view of the bridge, but from where he could see what was happening. In the space of half an hour he saw two trucks cross from the Hungarian side and one from the Austrian side. There were also a couple of pedestrians. The soldiers on duty seemed to know everyone who crossed. They chatted to the truck drivers and pedestrians. At one point a soldier from the Austrian side walked across the bridge to talk to the two on the Hungarian side. It seemed to Franz that the soldiers were very bored, and controls weren't too strict. He decided to risk it. At worst he could expect a few weeks in a military jail if he was stopped and arrested.

He saw the two soldiers on the Hungarian side get some bread and bottles out of their packs and start to eat. It was just after noon.

He strolled towards the bridge. As he was getting near to it a truck came from the Hungarian side and stopped at the first barrier. He was soon standing behind it. A soldier came out, raised the barrier, and waved the truck through. Franz walked past the sentry box. He nodded to the soldiers, who were both eating, said, "Hello", and carried on walking. He was in his Hungarian soldier's uniform. He expected them to call him back. The soldiers looked at each other for a moment, then returned to their food. They thought he was just a soldier who wanted to have a look at the other side of the border.

The truck had stopped at the other side. The driver had got out and was talking to one of the soldiers. Franz could not see the other soldier at all. He squeezed past the truck on the opposite side to the sentry box, ducked under the barrier and carried on walking. He had made it. He walked a hundred yards or so down the lane, and turned into a field on his left. He quickly took off his Hungarian soldier's uniform and put on his civilian jumper and trousers. He left the uniform in the field.

He walked on down the lane. He wanted to get some distance away from the border as quickly as possible. Soon he reached a main road. There was the occasional truck, and he decided to try to thumb a lift. He knew that he wanted to go north, back to Klaus's farm. A truck stopped and he got a lift to the town of Eisenstadt. Now he knew where he was, and which road to take in the direction of Jahrndorf. It took him three more lifts, and a lot of walking, but at half past eight in the evening he arrived at the farmhouse.

Klaus was amazed to see him. He took him inside, and his wife got Franz some bread and a drink.

Klaus had no idea what had happened to Franz. Since Franz disappeared over three months previously he had received no word. He didn't think that Franz had just decided to leave without saying anything, because his belongings were still in his room. He had wondered if he had been caught crossing the border.

Franz told him his story.

Klaus listened in amazement.

"Well, I don't know what we are going to do with you now. You are tired, and I need to think about it. Sleep now, and we will talk in the morning."

The following morning the discussion continued.

"Franz, you will be eighteen in a couple of weeks. Do you have any idea what you want to do with your life?"

"I'm not sure, but I think I need to move to another area. Perhaps it is time I tried something different from farming. I want to see if there is anything else I can do. Maybe one day I can have a farm of my own. I will never have that here. Your children will always come first. I think I will go west, maybe back to Germany. I will just see what turns up."

"I have a cousin in Salzburg," said Klaus. "He has a lumber business. There is big demand for wood. I can give you a letter to introduce you to him, if you like."

"Why not? It's worth a try. Thanks for everything, Klaus."

So Franz packed his few belongings, gathered together what was left of the profits he had made from smuggling cigarettes, and caught the bus to Vienna.

# Chapter Six

PETER MOSER, HAVING crossed the border illegally into Austria, made his way to Vienna by hitching rides on a series of trucks, farm vehicles, or whatever else was going in the right direction.

Since he did not have any papers he decided he had better report to the police station in the centre of the city. He knew that he would not be sent back to Hungary, but did not want to be stopped without valid documents, which might mean a jail sentence. In any case, he wanted to get the papers, which would allow him to go to Germany.

The policeman at the desk was used to refugees coming in to ask for help.

"You will have to register. We will take you to the registration office. It is run by the Three-Power Occupation Council."

A policeman was summoned to accompany Peter. They walked across the centre of the city, which was still heavily scarred by bombed-out buildings and piles of rubble.

The registration office was in a large three-storey building with its entrance in a narrow alleyway. The entrance hall was large but gloomy. Peter was taken to the desk where the policeman with him spoke briefly to the man in British soldier uniform who sat with a pile of papers in front of him. A second soldier was standing behind the desk. He came round the desk and indicated that Peter should follow him down a corridor to the left-hand side. The soldier motioned to Peter to sit on a bench at the far end of the corridor. There were two men and a woman already sitting on the bench waiting.

He sat there for almost two hours, until his turn came. He was shown into a small room. A British officer sat behind the desk. To the side of the desk sat another man in civilian dress. The officer said something in English, and the other man translated into German.

Peter was questioned in detail about his identity, where he came from, and why he had come into Austria illegally. The officer was obviously aware of the situation of ethnic Germans in post-war Eastern Europe, but he was particularly keen to know where Peter had been, and what he had done during the war. After fifty minutes of this questioning, slowed down by the translator having to repeat everything, there was a pause. The officer had been taking notes, which he quickly re-read. He lit a cigarette, and gazed at Peter as he took a long drag.

"Right," he said at last. He spoke quickly with the interpreter trying to keep up when the officer paused for breath. "You will be given papers to allow you to go to Germany, but not yet. You have broken the law by entering Austria illegally, and without papers. You and thousands of others. There aren't enough jails to put you all in, so the authorities have decided a standard sentence. You will be allocated a workplace for the next three months where you will work without pay, but you will have a bed and be fed. At the end of three months you will be given documents and put on a train into Germany, so long as you behave yourself and do the work you are given. Next!"

Peter was escorted out of the room, up a flight of stairs to another office. Thankfully, he found there was no waiting there.

The man in civilian clothes at the desk spoke to him in German.

"What work experience do you have?"

Peter thought fast. He didn't want anything that was going to be hard work, such as in a mine or on a building site. Just the thought of having to help clear the rubble he had seen in the city made him wince. He didn't want to be too closely supervised, which he would be in a factory or a workshop.

"I used to be a farm worker," he said. This was partly true, because before the war he had sometimes helped his mother and father in their field, but in reality he had little knowledge of the depth and variety of farm work. He knew though that it would be difficult for him to be supervised all the time on a farm.

So he spent the next three months on a farm a few miles to the north-east of Vienna. He did as little work as he thought he could get away with without his being referred back to the authorities in power, and at the end of the three months the farmer and his wife weren't sorry to see him go.

He went back to the registration office. His photo was taken and a day later he was able to collect identification papers. He was told to report to the train station at seven a.m. the following morning.

After a final night in the refugees' hostel he went to the station before seven in the morning. There was a group of about twenty men and women all waiting for the train. Two hours later the train arrived. It was already packed with refugees. About a dozen were allowed to get off, and they were taken to two ambulances, which had been waiting in the station yard. Two American soldiers checked the papers of each of those waiting, before allowing them onto the train. Red Cross workers passed food packets and bottles of water to the refugees through the train windows. After an hour's wait the train set off.

At Munich the train stopped again. An extra carriage was added, which had a doctor and two nurses aboard. The train now made better speed. By late evening it had arrived at Stuttgart. Here the train was split into two. Peter's journey finally ended when the train pulled into Karlsruhe station at just after three a.m. in the morning.

The guards told everyone they would have to stay on the train until seven-thirty a.m. Peter tried to get a little sleep. It was now the middle of February 1946, and the temperature was well below zero.

The disembarkation process took until mid-afternoon to complete. Peter was given vouchers for food and accommodation, and told which bus to get on for the short ride to the camp.

This was an ex-prisoner-of-war-camp, similar to all the wooden sheds hurriedly erected in many parts of Germany during the war. It had the usual dormitories crammed with bunks, crowded, with no privacy, and a constant queue for the few toilets and wash basins. He needed to get out of this as soon as possible.

Peter soon found temporary work. Karlsruhe is situated on the Rhine in south-western Germany, not far from the French border, and about forty-five miles west of Stuttgart. It had been bombed and ravaged by the war like most German cities. There was still a lot of clearing and building work to be done. It wasn't to Peter's liking, but he had no choice.

He noticed that the refugees were gradually being moved from the camp, to be replaced by new arrivals. He went to the camp office to ask when he could be moved out into a flat or house.

"You are free to go whenever you want, but I don't think you will find anywhere, unless you have a lot of money, that is. There are far more refugees than we can find housing for. More accommodation is being built, but it will be a long time before there will be enough to take everybody. We are making the local people give up any spare rooms in their houses to take refugees. Families and couples are given priority. You will have to wait until things improve."

This was not what Peter wanted to hear.

He thought long and hard about what to do next. He decided to try to get in touch with two of the girlfriends he had spent time with during the war. One or other of them might be willing to take him in, assuming, of course, that they had survived and that the war hadn't left them homeless. There was Inge in Berlin, and Renate in Düsseldorf. He wrote virtually the same letter to each of them, telling them where he was, and asking about their own situations.

Whilst he waited and hoped for replies to his letters he worked as a labourer. It was not what he wanted, but he was desperate for money. Every day builders came to the camp looking for workers, so finding temporary work wasn't a problem. He saved as much as he could.

Ten days after sending off the letters he got a reply from Inge Braun. She was still at the same flat in Berlin, in the western zone. Her letter was enthusiastic, almost begging him to go see her. He didn't need much persuading. He remembered that he had enjoyed some very steamy sex sessions with Inge. All the more reason to go to her.

He wrote back to her saying he was on his way.

Two days later he made the complicated journey, which took him into West Berlin. Since Berlin was well inside the Russian-occupied zone of Germany there was only one route into the western sector of the City, and it took him a full day's travelling to get there. The journey took him through several more German cities, which had been devastated by Allied bombing. It was April 1946, over a year after the end of the war in Europe, but large areas of many of the cities were still full of ruined buildings and mountains of rubble. Reconstruction had started but there was a tremendous amount of work to be done, which would take several years to complete.

Once in Berlin, Peter caught the tram from the station to the street where Inge lived. Half the buildings had been destroyed, and all had damage of some kind. He went into the block of flats and up the stairs to Inge's flat. He knocked on the door. She opened it and threw her arms round his neck, kissing him passionately.

For a while they didn't speak much. He could see she hadn't changed. She was still pretty, twenty-seven years old, tall and slim with dark, wavy hair. She made a simple meal of sausage and sauerkraut, and had managed to get hold of a bottle of wine from somewhere.

They ate and drank the wine. They began to relate the events that had taken place in the two years since they had last met.

She had been in Berlin the whole time. The bombing and firestorms had been horrendous. She had almost starved to death, but at least she had survived. Somehow the bombs had missed the block of flats. The worst part was the shooting in the streets as the Russians fought their way into the city. For several days nobody dared to go outside. There had been no food, and the water and electricity supplies were off for days on end. She had seen her elderly next-door neighbour shot in the street below when she had gone to try to get food.

He asked her if she had suffered when the Russian soldiers arrived.

She wept. "Every woman who looked half decent was raped, a lot of us many times, over a period of three months."

They sat in silence for a long time after the meal was finished.

She got up, looked into his eyes, took his hand and said, "Peter, let's go to bed now."

The next morning they talked about the future.

Inge was working as a waitress in a bar used mostly by American and English servicemen.

"I hate it there. Someone is always trying to paw me. The Americans think they can buy anything with cigarettes and a packet of nylons."

"I need to find work to get some money," said Peter.

"You won't find anything here. This side of Berlin is overflowing with people because everybody wants to live in the western zone. You can't leave Berlin unless you travel back to the west. There isn't enough work for the people who already live here."

Peter was disappointed. They talked about the situation for several hours.

At length Peter said, "Do you have any money saved?"

"I don't get much pay, but if I am nice to them the Americans give good tips. Why?"

"I can get work in Karlsruhe," said Peter, "and I'm sure you would find a job. We would have to find somewhere to live, but it's easier for a couple than for me on my own."

"Let me think about it," said Inge. "I have a job here, and somewhere to live, but I can't support two of us. You can stay to try to find a job. If you can't we will have to think again."

Peter and Inge lived together in her flat for the next five weeks. Inge was often able to bring home small amounts of leftover snack foods from the bar where she worked. Peter preferred this to anything Inge prepared herself. She was not a good cook, and in any case it was almost impossible to buy meat. Most of the time the people were living on boiled potatoes. Ration books were issued to everyone who had papers, but the food supposedly to be bought on ration was rarely available in the shops. It was too easy to divert food supplies to the black market.

Only poor quality food was available in the shops. Some of the occupying troops, particularly the Americans, were running nice little businesses on the side. There were always people with money prepared to buy at inflated prices, or more likely, to barter their personal possessions for food.

Peter went out most days to look for work. He got occasional work as a labourer, but most of the time he could find nothing.

Sometimes he went to the bar where Inge worked. A few of the Americans could speak German, and they asked him why he went there, to a bar full of foreigners.

He told them that he lived with Inge, and that he couldn't find work. He was thinking of going back to Karlsruhe. Maybe he could find permanent work as a locksmith, which was the trade for which he had been trained when he first left school. He knew there would be better chance of more regular work there, but he had to convince Inge that she would get a job if she went with him.

One of the Americans who visited the bar regularly was in charge of the army catering in Berlin. He said he knew the man in charge of catering in Karlsruhe. He would get in touch with him to see if there were any jobs available.

Peter thought no more of it. It was just talk, and the Americans always had plenty to say, even if he couldn't understand most of it.

By the end of July 1946, Peter was becoming very frustrated because he couldn't find regular work in Berlin. One day he went to the bar as usual, where he was approached by the American catering manager, who was looking pleased with himself.

"Hi! I've got some good news for you. Our man in Karlsruhe says he has got an opening for a waitress in the officers' mess. Does Inge want the job?"

Inge and Peter discussed the situation. She knew he was thinking of leaving her to go back to Karlsruhe by himself. She didn't want to risk losing him.

"If I go with you, will we get married?"

Peter wasn't so sure. This was the first time in his life he had been with just one woman for any length of time. But maybe it was time to give marriage a try.

"Yes, sure, as soon as we get settled in Karlsruhe," he replied.

A week later they were on the train. From the station in Karlsruhe they went straight to the American Army barracks to see the catering manager, Jake.

"Where are you two staying?" was his first question.

"We have to find somewhere," replied Peter.

"Hmm. Maybe I can help you. Would you be bothered where it was, or if it wasn't very big?"

"Believe me," said Peter, "just about anything will be better than the refugee camp. But how can you find something when every room is already taken, and people are having to sleep four in one room?"

"Contacts. The currency I deal in is tins of corned beef, cigarettes, chocolate, nylons, you name it. It's better than money in this town. If anybody wants anything, come and see me first. I'll have to speak to a couple of people. There's a storeroom you can sleep in tonight. Bit uncomfortable, but I should have some news tomorrow."

Their first night in Karlsruhe was spent on the floor of the tiny storeroom at the back of the kitchens. They had to be up at five, because the cooks came in to work at half past.

Peter sat in the corner of the canteen whilst Jake showed Inge what her work would involve, which didn't take long.

They couldn't wait there, so Jake told them to come back at two in the afternoon.

When they returned Jake was in his office with a well-dressed German.

The German asked them if they had any money. Inge had saved a few dollars, given to her by Americans as tips, and they had some marks. The German took the dollars, but told them the marks were worthless. He said this was a deposit on a flat. Jake nodded reassuringly. They left with the German. He took them out to his car, and drove for less than five minutes to a street of high buildings, the ground floors of which were mostly shops, though none of them had much on display in the windows to sell.

They picked their way across the rubble to go through a large door between two of the shop entrances, and climbed up a staircase to the second storey of the building. The German opened a door in the back corner of the landing, and they went inside. There was one room containing an old bed and a wardrobe. A door led off to a tiny kitchen, with a stove and a sink. Another door led to an equally tiny room, which was just big enough to take a "half bath" and a toilet. Not brilliant by any means, but paradise compared with the conditions that most of the people in the city were having to put up with at the time.

They settled in and Inge started to work in the canteen.

Peter still couldn't find a permanent job, but sometimes he would be taken on for several weeks at a time, and most of the time he had work. He was able to do occasional work as a locksmith, his original trade, but he knew he didn't want to do that for the rest of his life. Anything that tied him to a regular place of work, or regular hours, didn't attract him.

He went to the army canteen sometimes to meet Inge at the end of her shift, and he became quite friendly with Jake. Sometimes it was useful for the Americans to have a driver who could speak German, and he got jobs driving American officials around, on a casual basis.

He began to act as a middleman, making a little money by getting things for people, which weren't normally available, using first of all Jake, and then Jake's contacts to locate the things he was looking for. He didn't make a lot of money, but it certainly improved his and Inge's lifestyle.

# Chapter Seven

PETER WROTE TO his mother, Anna, in Nagymányok, to tell her that he was in Karlsruhe, and had found a flat to live in. He didn't mention that he was living with Inge. The old man still lived in the house in Nagymányok, which Anna and Victoria had been forced to leave, and he forwarded the letter to Anna at the butcher's in Szárász.

When Peter got the reply telling him that the family had had to split up, and that they had lost their house and just about all their possessions, he was shocked.

He wrote back to Anna in Szárász. He said that he thought they should come to Karlsruhe. Things were good there, and improving all the time.

Anna went to see Reiner in Dombóvár to show him Peter's letter. They discussed the situation.

Reiner said, "Well, we don't seem to have much future here. Everybody hates the Germans. Everything we had has been taken from us. Nobody will give me a job, and I am fed up of always being afraid that someone will tell the police I am here. What do we have to lose by going to Germany?"

What indeed? It would be difficult for the family's situation to be any worse.

In October 1946 they made plans to leave.

They faced the same predicament as Peter, no papers or authorisation to get them out of Hungary or into Germany. Reiner would be arrested if he applied for papers. Anna knew from stories of other Germans who had left that it was possible to pay for a guide to take them over the border into Austria.

She went to Vasas to collect Victoria from her sister Eva's house. The sisters wept as they said goodbye. They didn't know if they would ever see each other again.

Anna and Victoria went back to the butcher's in Szárász where Anna put together the few clothes and belongings they would be able to carry with them.

The following morning they left to join Reiner at his aunt's in Dombóvár. They stayed overnight, and early the next morning there were more tearful farewells as the three of them set off west on the first of three bus journeys which took them by late afternoon to the town of Körmend, less than three miles from the Austrian border.

The town was quite busy in the centre. They knew they had to find someone to take them over the border, but they had no idea where to find such a person. They had no need to worry. The sight of strangers walking in the town carrying packs of belongings was quite common. When they got near to the end of the main street a man beckoned them into a small side street. They followed him round to the back of a yard where they stopped under a lean-to built onto a barn.

He spoke to them in Hungarian.

"You want to cross the border?"

Reiner spoke for the three of them, since his mother's Hungarian was very poor.

"Yes, can you help us?"

They discussed the price. Once that was agreed the Hungarian asked them if they had any Austrian money.

"No, none at all," said Reiner, "but we have a little Hungarian money left."

"I can take it off you and give you some Austrian," said the man.

So another deal was made, at a very poor rate of exchange from the family's point of view, but having some Austrian money would help a lot once they were over the border, and Hungarian money was going to be of no use whatsoever.

"Meet me back here when it gets dark," said the man, and disappeared down the street.

They walked around side and back streets to try to keep warm, and they ate some bread and cooked meat, which the butcher had given Anna when they left.

It was soon dark and they met the man as arranged. He was now wearing boots, had a small pack strapped to his back, and carried a long walking stick.

"I hope you are all fit," he said as he motioned them to follow him across a field.

This man had obviously made the journey more than once before. He knew where the best ground was for walking, and where the farm gates and fences were.

They were soon climbing through some woods on a narrow trail. Before long he motioned them to stop before they entered a cleared strip of land, about twenty yards wide, which crossed their route at right angles. He stood there in silence for a good two minutes, listening for any noise. Then he quickly crossed the clearing to a barbed wire fence with the others following close behind.

Victoria was afraid. How could they climb the fence?

The man carefully placed the handle of his long stick under the fence and with a quick pull opened a gap large enough for one person to get through. He pushed them through the gap, and then followed, pulling the barbed wire back into place behind him. Once more the fence looked as if it was an unbroken continuous stretch.

They continued to climb through the woods and soon picked up another trail. Now there was a thin covering of snow on the ground, the first fall of the coming winter, which got deeper as they climbed higher into the hills.

Their feet were soon wet, and Victoria wished she had the man's boots, even if they were several sizes too big for her.

At least the snow helped them to pick out the landscape better. They were heading for a gap in the mountains ahead, and after another half an hour reached the summit of the ridge. A few yards further on they picked up the beginnings of a small stream, which ran down the small valley in front of them.

The man stopped.

"Right, this is as far as I go. If you follow this stream down it joins a farm track. After about half an hour's walking you will pass the hamlet of Urbersdorf. Then it becomes a road in the same direction for another half hour to the village of Güssing. Do you know where you are heading for?"

"No," said Reiner. "We will go to the nearest big town and report to the police."

"I wouldn't do that if I were you," said the man. "This is the Russian zone, and if they catch you they might send you back into Hungary, or put you into jail. The Austrians hate the Russians, so they won't turn you in, but you need to go north to the American zone. There is an early morning Post bus, which will take you from Güssing to St Johann. From there you can get another bus to Neunkirchen in the American zone. Ten miles to the west of there is the main refugee registration centre at Gloggnitz. Good luck."

He walked back the way they had come, leaving them standing in the snow.

They ate some of the bread, which was left over, and carried on walking down into the valley. They didn't see a soul as they walked through the silent landscape. It was a beautiful night, but they were very tired and their feet were cold and wet, so they were not in any mood to appreciate the scenery.

Their guide's directions were good. They arrived at Güssing and found what looked to be the place where the bus turned round. There was no snow at this lower level. At first light the little bus arrived. There were no passengers, but the driver got off and delivered a bag to a nearby house, which looked as if it was the village shop. He gave them a long, hard look as they got on, but didn't say anything, other than when he told them the cost of the fare to St Johann.

A few passengers got on during the journey, but none of them spoke to the three of them.

St. Johann was no bigger than Güssing, but it was on a main road, and there was an hourly bus service to Neunkirchen. After ten minutes a bus arrived. This carried a number of passengers and was driven by an old man. He spoke quietly to Anna as she got on.

"Are you heading for Gloggnitz?"

"Yes," replied Anna.

"Have you got the papers for when we cross from the Russian to the American zones?"

"No, we don't have any papers."

"The Russians will want to see everyone's papers when we reach the boundary. You will have to get off when I tell you."

They had little choice but to go on the bus. As it approached a small village the driver stopped and called Reiner forward.

"You will have to get off here. You see that farm track on the left. Go down it and turn right through the farmyard. Go through the gate and across the field path round the hill. You will come out back on the road."

They did as they were told. As they walked through the farmyard a young boy came out of the farmhouse and showed them the way. Once round the hill he checked that the coast was clear, and then pointed the way down to a gate to the road. The bus arrived almost at the same time as they did, having been delayed for five minutes at the checkpoint. The driver smiled as they climbed back on. This had obviously happened more than once before.

The rest of the journey passed without incident. They caught another bus in Neunkirchen for the ten-mile journey to Gloggnitz. They hadn't slept for two days, and Victoria fell asleep on the bus. They got off the bus in the centre of the town. There was a group of American soldiers in the square. They had guns, but were just standing together smoking and chatting. It was obvious to them that the new arrivals were refugees. One of the soldiers came over and pointed to one of the streets leading off a corner of the square. Fifty yards down the street a track led off into a yard with a wooden hut, which had an American flag on its roof. A soldier on guard duty motioned them inside.

Now they had to go through an interrogation session, or so they thought. But it was late in the afternoon, and the men in uniforms behind the desk had had enough for one day.

The family was taken through to the camp behind the hut, where there were a row of five larger huts. A guard took them into a hut and pointed out three empty bunks in different parts of the hut. They had beds and shelter for the night.

The next morning they were able to wash and clean themselves up a little. They went to one of the other huts, which served as a communal eating room, where there were long wooden tables and benches. Here they queued for a bowl of soup, and were given a piece of bread each. The room was full of other refugees, and it was noisy, but the hot soup tasted wonderful after two days without proper food or anything warm to eat or drink.

Then they were taken back to the hut at the entrance to the camp. They had to sit with a group of a dozen refugees who had arrived during the night, until it was their turn.

The interrogation followed the same pattern as that

which Peter had gone through a few months earlier, and the result was also the same. They were illegal immigrants into Austria and would have to work for no pay for three months before they would be allowed to continue their journey.

Before they were allocated a workplace they were told to go to the Austrian council offices in the village to be issued with identity cards.

They stayed at the camp for two more nights. Then they were told to get their belongings together to be ready to leave at eight a.m. the following morning.

They were put on an American army bus, along with several other refugees.

To the west of Gloggnitz lies an area of mountains, divided by wooded valleys, with the highest peaks over 6,000ft. This is a local holiday area for the people of Vienna, and there are hotels dotted around the valleys. The family was put off the bus outside a hotel in the Raxalpe region. The owners of the hotel were expecting them, and came out to meet the bus. They told Anna that she and Victoria would work in their hotel. Reiner was to go with another man who was waiting there. He was the owner of a hotel ten minutes' walk away, and Reiner would be working for him.

So the family settled in to a routine of work. They didn't mind this at all, after what they had been through since the end of the war. They had nice beds to sleep in, and enjoyed good food. The work was no problem at all, and the owners were quite sympathetic.

Anna worked as a cook in the kitchens. Victoria was a chambermaid, and served at table at mealtimes. Reiner worked as a porter and handyman at the other hotel. They worked hard and were well regarded by the owners. They weren't paid, but customers gave Victoria small tips for serving at table, and she saved this money. The winter snows set in, so the skiing season was beginning, and there was a steady stream of visitors who stayed mostly for a week at a time. Even in the years just after the end of the war there were still people in Vienna with enough money to be able to holiday in a hotel.

Anna wrote to Peter in Karlsruhe to tell him where they were. He replied saying that when the three months were over they should join him in Karlsruhe. The situation there was improving all the time, and the future looked much better.

Early in March 1947 it was time for them to leave. They would have liked to stay, but the hotel owners couldn't afford to pay full wages to Anna and Reiner. The owner said to Victoria that if she decided to come back when she was older she could have a job.

They packed their few belongings together and caught the bus back down the valley to Gloggnitz. They went back to the office at the camp. The officer in charge filled out a piece of paper and gave it to Reiner. "Take this to the station. This will get you tickets to Passau. When you get there you will be taken to the refugee registration centre."

They set off to the station from where they caught a local train to Vienna. They had to wait at the station in Vienna for over two hours before catching the train for Germany. The line followed the Danube valley west to the city of Linz, and then meandered through some low hills to the German border. Passau is situated right on the border, on the German side.

Unfortunately the last part of the journey was through a Russian zone. The train stopped near to a small village just before the border where soldiers got on to check everyone's papers. This shouldn't have been a problem, but what the three of them didn't realise was that the brown identity cards they had been issued were only good for travel within the Austrian borders. In order to leave Austria they needed blue identity cards, and they hadn't been issued with those.

There was no arguing with the Russian soldiers. The family couldn't continue across the border on the train, and were made to get off. They stood at the side of the track and watched as the train pulled away. Reiner decided they had better get away from there before the Russian soldiers tried to arrest them, or made any plans to have them sent back.

The village nearby was basically a few houses around a crossroads, several of them being farmhouses. It was rare for anyone to get off the trains, when they had been stopped for inspection. As they stood at the crossroads in a steady drizzle, not knowing what to do next, an old man came up to them.

"Problems with your papers?" he asked.

"Yes," replied Reiner. "We have the wrong kind of identity cards."

"It's not far to the border from here," said the man. "It's fairly easy to get across if you go the right way. I can show you, but there are Russian soldiers on an exercise tonight. It would have to be tomorrow night."

"Is there anywhere we can stay tonight?" asked Anna.

"I don't have any space, but the farmer over there might help you."

He pointed down a track to a farmyard.

"Meet me back here at seven tomorrow evening."

They followed the track to the farm. Reiner went to knock on the door.

The farmer himself opened the door. Reiner explained their predicament, and asked if there was somewhere they could sleep for the night.

"I want to help you," said the farmer, "but there is a law now which says that we mustn't help refugees. They are getting to be very strict about it. I am due in court next week for helping other refugees. They will probably make me pay a fine. I am very sorry, but I can't help you."

The three turned away dejected, and started to walk slowly back across the yard towards the track. As they passed a large barn, a man beckoned them towards him.

"Are you looking for somewhere to stay for the night?"

Reiner explained what had happened, and that they were desperate for somewhere to sleep.

"Well, perhaps I can help you. I work here. My room is on a landing at the back of this barn. You can stay there provided you keep out of sight. The farmer never goes up to my room. Come, follow me."

The room was small but homely. Warm and dry. There was just one bed.

"You can sleep here," said the man. "I can sleep in the straw for one night."

They couldn't get over this man's kindness. Not many

would give up their room and bed for three bedraggled strangers.

Anna and Victoria slept in the bed. Reiner managed to make himself quite comfortable on the floor. Victoria said later that this was the best night's sleep she ever had.

The next morning the man gave them some bread and coffee.

He made sure the farmer wasn't around before taking them down to the road.

They thanked him profusely for what he had done for them. It made them feel more positive about the future. Things were going to get better.

So once again, in freezing conditions, the three of them had to cross a border illegally in darkness. As the old man had said, it wasn't difficult so long as you knew where to avoid the patrols of Russian soldiers. There were no mountains here, only fields and farms. The man knew the terrain well. They seemed to go in several different directions, following tracks and paths across the farmland. After a couple of hours, the old man stopped and said to them, "Welcome to Germany." They were surprised, as they hadn't seen anything to indicate the border.

He pointed to a narrow road, and they could see in the distance the dim lights of a town.

"Passau," said the man. "This is where I leave you."

Reiner offered the man some money, though they had little left. He refused to take anything.

"You will need everything you've got. Goodbye and good luck."

The family thanked him and each shook his hand. They turned to walk down the road to the town of Passau.

It was still dark when they arrived. There was little sign of life. They were suffering from the cold and there was an icy breeze, so they huddled together under a lean-to out of the wind to wait for daylight.

As it began to get light the town began to stir itself, and a few people appeared on the streets. Reiner stopped a passer-by and asked for directions to the gathering centre for refugees. The woman pointed out the way but said that there could be a problem.

"Why?" asked Reiner.

"Because today is Sunday, and all government and council-run offices are shut. That will almost certainly apply to the gathering centre."

They made their way to the centre. There was a notice on the door saying that the centre office was closed for Sunday as usual.

Not everything was closed. With almost the last of their money they managed to buy some freshly baked bread and cheese, and a hot drink from a snack stall at the side of the market place. But what were they going to do for the rest of the day, and where could they sleep for the night?

The day was spent trudging around the streets of Passau trying to find somewhere to sleep. There wasn't a spare bed in the town. The locals were sympathetic to the refugees, but they were unhappy that the centre had been put in their town, because there was a constant stream of strangers trudging the streets and stopping them from going about their normal business. These refugees often had no money and many resorted to begging, and the locals didn't like it.

As it started to get dark Anna decided that they weren't

going to find anywhere to stay, and she decided that they would go to the police station for help.

The man behind the desk looked at the three cold and weary travellers standing in front of him. His duty was clear to him.

"You will have to stay in the jail tonight. You are not allowed to wander round town."

So the family spent their first night in Germany in Passau's police station jail.

Reiner was put in a cell with other men.

Anna and Victoria were put in the women's cell. The cells were meant to take one or two inmates only on an overnight basis. They were very small with a couple of rough bunks. There was no running water supply. There was just a large bowl of water and a tin mug. The toilet was a bucket in the corner. It was soon full.

There were twenty women including Anna and Victoria. They tried to find a space on the floor to sleep, using their baggage as pillows, but there wasn't enough room to stretch out. Sleep was impossible. One of the women was on the edge of a breakdown. She was moaning to herself, then shouting out, then screaming. Nobody could calm her. Victoria thought this was the worst night of her life, so far.

They were glad to leave the jail the following morning.

Reiner too had managed to get very little sleep.

Two policemen took all the refugees to the gathering centre. It wasn't open yet, but already there were about fifty people waiting outside the door. It was going to be a long wait.

When it was finally their turn, they were asked why

their identification cards were wrong. Anna related the whole story. The man behind the desk said he would arrange for new German identity cards to be issued. It would take two days. He said they would have to stay in a nearby camp until train seats became available. Anna produced the latest letter from Peter.

"My other son is in Karlsruhe. We would like to go to him."

The man quickly glanced through the letter.

"Yes. I can give you tickets for Karlsruhe. You might have to wait an extra day for the train though."

They went to the camp in Passau. It also had been a prisoner-of-war camp. Conditions were cramped, but adequate for a few days. They were fed and could get a wash. All they could do was wait.

On the afternoon of the third day they were told that their train would leave early the following morning.

The train left soon after daybreak. It was packed with people. Most had to stand, but a few hardy individuals sat up on the roof, even though it was bitterly cold. The train went slowly, first to Munich, then Augsburg, Ulm and Stuttgart.

The family had not seen any bombing in Hungary. Vienna had been badly bombed, with piles of rubble everywhere, but as they passed through the centres of these German cities they couldn't believe the extent of the destruction. Whole areas were flattened. Other parts had remains of walls, chimneys, and spires pointing up to the sky in jagged formations like huge fields of stalagmites. The centres of these cities were completely ruined. As a priority the railway tracks had been rebuilt, and the major roads were passable, but the rest was just a mess, even though it was almost two years since the end of the war in Europe.

"Come to Germany," Peter had written to Anna, "things are improving all the time. There is a future for us here."

"Why did we leave Austria?" Anna thought to herself.

As the train finally pulled into Karlsruhe in the late afternoon they could see that this too had suffered a lot of damage from the bombs. Peter's letter had said that things were good here, but the reality shocked them. Out of the frying pan into the fire?

It took a long time for the train to unload its human cargo. Several buses started taking full loads of refugees to the former army barracks, which now served as first accommodation for new arrivals. Once more they were allocated bunks and tried to settle in. Too many people were crammed in, but there was no choice. Certainly there was no privacy, but they were fed and had somewhere dry and warm to sleep. With a bit of luck they wouldn't be there long.

The next morning they set off to find Peter. He didn't know they were coming, but they had the address.

It was a Sunday morning, so they hoped he would be there.

Peter opened the door of the flat. There were a few tears all round as the family members hugged each other. There had been times when each of them had thought this moment would never come.

Anna saw a tall young woman with dark hair standing behind Peter. She was obviously pregnant.

Peter stood aside.

"This is my wife, Inge."

There was no room for Peter and Inge to accommodate the rest of the family in their tiny flat. So for the next few weeks the three new arrivals had to live in the barracks. It was overcrowded and noisy, the bunks were hard, small and stacked too closely together. Every day there were new arrivals, and a few moved out. The family would just have to wait their turn.

The authorities had little choice but to force the local population to give up any spare rooms to the incoming refugees. Most of them hated the thought of taking in refugees, and made sure the refugees were aware of their opposition.

After a few weeks Anna, Reiner and Victoria were sent to live with a woman who had a house with two spare rooms. Her husband and son had been killed in the war. She didn't want to take in refugees, and she was extremely unpleasant to them. They were told that they weren't to use the toilet and bathroom without asking her permission first. They could use the kitchen only when she had finished her work in there. She spoke to them only when absolutely necessary. They mustn't make any noise, play any music, or have any visitors. They hoped they would soon find somewhere permanent to live.

They stayed there over the winter of 1947/48.

Early in 1948 Inge had a baby boy. She had to stop work. Luckily there was plenty of work available for Peter. There was a massive building programme, which meant that Reiner was also fully employed using his carpenter's skills.

The immediate priority was to carry on clearing the devastated areas and rebuild the city centre. Large numbers of the original population had lost their homes, but there were also a huge number of refugees to be housed, with more arriving every day. There was no time to build houses in the traditional ways. Blocks of land were appropriated for the construction of rows of single-storey wooden terrace houses.

The family hoped to be allocated one of these homes, but there was a very long waiting list. They wanted to get away from the nasty woman.

Rebuilding was gathering pace, financed by American money. The German economy, like the rest of Europe, was in a shambles. Rationing was stricter than it had been during most of the war. The situation was made worse by the constant stream of refugees from the east, both those evicted by the Communist authorities, and those who chose to leave. There was plenty of money around, but it was the old German mark, considered worthless by everyone. The authorities strictly controlled the prices of essential goods, which meant that there was little or nothing to buy in the shops. Everything had to be bartered, and the black market flourished. For someone like Peter the situation was ideal. He accumulated lots of goods, and his American connections helped him considerably.

The chaotic financial situation was mostly resolved in June 1948, when the authorities replaced the old German mark with the D-Mark. At the same time almost all price controls were removed. The authorities had managed to keep the impending change mostly secret, in order not to cause panic. Every adult German was given forty D-Mark in exchange for forty old marks, but anything over that was negotiable. The immediate effect was that one new D-Mark became worth fifteen old marks, and the old currency rapidly disappeared. Suddenly goods appeared in the shops, many of which had only been available on the black market. Prices were fixed by supply, demand and competition. In other words, free market conditions took over. The small number of people who had land, property, or goods of value gained considerably from the change. Those with their assets in the form of old marks lost out, but from that point on the economy started to stabilise and improve.

Anna didn't work. She had been through a lot in the last four years. Her husband was dead. Her sons had gone to war, and she had been afraid they would not return. She had hidden them from the new authorities, always fearing the knock on the door, which would mean their being taken away. At the age of forty-eight she found herself in a new country, itself devastated by war, having to try to re-build her life. She suffered from dreadful nightmares. She awoke screaming, "Don't let them take me away!" She had no useful training to enable her to find a job. She didn't want or feel capable of physical hard work, which was mostly what was available. She did the cleaning and cooking for Reiner and Victoria.

Victoria had not been able to go to school since they left Hungary. Her education had been elementary, and virtually non-existent after her twelfth birthday. She was able to speak German and Hungarian, but the latter was going to be of little use in the future. She would be fifteen in October 1948, and there was no point in her trying to resume her studies. She was interested in dressmaking and applied for a job as a sewing machinist. There was to be a one-day trial without pay. If she were thought to be suitable she would be kept on.

The day was a disaster. There was one large room with over twenty young women working at the machines. The manageress was a tyrant. Nobody was allowed to speak unless spoken to. If anyone made a mistake, or wasn't working fast enough they were shouted at. The day lasted nine hours, and there was only one twenty-minute break at lunchtime. Victoria tried her best, but she was glad at the end of the day to be told she wasn't going to be offered a job.

Eventually Victoria was able to find work as a maid. There were still a few rich people around. The pay wasn't much for a young girl. This was the sort of work she did for the next few years. Sometimes she had cleaning jobs.

At one place where she worked as a cleaner the woman of the house ran a small dance school during the day, whilst her husband went out to work. Victoria would try to be working in or near the dance room when the lessons were taking place. After the students left she would try to practise the steps on her own, without any music. Although she was young, Victoria wasn't completely naïve. She realised that the young man who came in to teach dancing twice a week spent a lot of time with the woman proprietor, and what they were doing together had nothing to do with dance steps!

Victoria's years working in rich people's houses as a maid and cleaner taught her a lot about the way people lived. She observed their habits, and saw the way they cheated and lied to each other. Her experiences during these years helped to make her very cynical about people's behaviour and motives, cynicism which, if anything, grew over the years.

In the late 1940s it was estimated that over thirty per cent of the population of southern Germany consisted of refugees from the east. The percentage of refugees was much higher in the big cities. They had come from a number of different countries, but most were of German descent. Despite their having maintained a German culture in the lands they had been forced to leave, most of them were homesick. They had absorbed many of the traditions of their adopted countries in the period of over two hundred years that their families had lived there.

During the years following the end of the war, and in many cases into the 'fifties and beyond, associations were run by and for refugees who had come from the same areas in the east. There were many of these groups in the cities and towns where there were large numbers of refugees.

The groups held social gatherings where they would wear national dress and prepare the kind of food they had eaten in their homelands. Traditional music would be played at dances. There were even a number of films made depicting stories of a romanticised view of life in their former homelands. All of this was to try to make the refugees feel less homesick. Many of them would never return to the lands of their births, which they had been forced to leave.

Anna was a little older than many of the other refugees. There were a number of others living nearby who had come from Hungary. These people regarded Anna as a mother figure, and would come to her with their problems, or just to talk about the old times in Hungary.

That their mother had come to be regarded as "Mother Hungary" amused Reiner and Victoria. They knew that Anna had difficulty in putting together even a simple sentence in Hungarian.

The family settled into a routine. They hoped that one day they would be able to move to a home of their own, but thousands of others in the area were in the same position. They had somewhere to live, there was work for Reiner and Victoria, and they earned enough to live on. They lived in the woman's flat for six years, through to 1953.

Perhaps it is unkind to say the woman who owned the flat was nasty to them. Put yourself in her position. Would you like it if you were forced to take three people you didn't know to live in your home for six years?

Reiner had a few girlfriends, but nobody on a long-term basis. He was perhaps overly critical, always looking for perfection in a woman. In his eyes perfection would be a woman who was a first-class cook and housekeeper.

Victoria made friends with other girls at the dances of the local Hungarian association, but she didn't have a regular boyfriend. At the age of nineteen, early in 1953, she had grown into an attractive dark-haired young woman. She had long ago changed her sparse eating habits, and would happily eat most kinds of food. She often helped her mother to cook, and had become very good at preparing meals.

The associations for former refugees became very well organised. Each one made lists of its members. These lists were circulated to other associations for the same country of origin, which had been set up in the cities and large towns of southern Germany. Friends and relatives were often able to re-establish contact as a result of these lists. Victoria found that some of her old schoolfriends were in other towns in Germany, and she was able to make contact and visit them.

The economic situation was beginning to improve, and at long last the people looked to the future with a little hope.

# Chapter Eight

SOMEHOW VIENNA DIDN'T appeal to Franz. In December 1948 it was still one big building site. As in all the cities there was work available in the building trade. Building something new was one thing, but helping to clear mountains of rubble wasn't to his liking. He decided to take Klaus's advice and move on to Salzburg.

He caught a train to Linz, and then he caught the next train leaving heading west, which took him to Salzburg. As he left the station there and began to look around he felt more cheerful. There were few of the after-effects of war to be seen here. The town looked attractive, even in the thin December sunshine. The people didn't look so war-weary, though he saw the occasional disabled ex-soldier as he walked the central area. He would see what it could offer him.

After walking round the centre of the town he decided it was time to find Klaus's cousin. He caught a bus to the village of Niederalm, a village in a wooded valley a few miles to the south of Salzburg. Franz asked a passer-by for directions. He walked up a road for half a mile towards a wooded hillside, and then into a large compound which had piles of felled tree trunks stacked around the sides. There was a lorry being loaded with tree trunks by means of a metal block hung from the spar of a small truck, from each end of which chains with grappling hooks were attached to the tree trunk. One man was driving the truck and two more were helping to secure the hooks to the trunks before they could be lifted, then removing them after the trunks had been put safely onto the lorry.

The men ignored Franz and carried on with the work. He stood and watched fascinated by the apparent ease with which the huge trunks could be lifted and accurately placed on the lorry. After ten minutes the lorry was full, the load was secured in place, and it drove off.

The man driving the truck got out and came over to Franz.

"Are you looking for somebody?"

"I'm looking for Werner."

"That's me. You don't look like someone who wants to buy a load of wood."

Franz smiled as he gave him the letter from Klaus.

Werner read it and then paused for a moment as he studied Franz.

"Well, I suppose I could use another pair of hands. It will be hard work, and I can't pay you much. You will need to find somewhere to stay. My house is too small for you to live with us, but there are some cheap places in the village offering rooms. Want to give it a try?"

"Yes, why not?" replied Franz. He liked the idea of doing something different from farming, and he would still be working in the open air. He also liked the idea of having the freedom of a place of his own, since he had always lived with family up to now, apart from when he was in the army in Hungary.

"Go back into the village to the square. At the side opposite the bridge there is an alleyway with two or three places near the far end which rent out rooms. If you can't find anything come back here. Otherwise you can start work tomorrow morning at seven. Bring some food for your dinner."

Werner was very direct. He was about fifty, much older than his cousin Klaus. He was thick-set and looked strong. Franz took an immediate liking to him.

Franz went to two of the houses down the alleyway mentioned by Werner, and found a small attic room in the second, at a rent he thought he could afford.

The next morning Werner and his employees began to show Franz how the logging business worked. There was a skill to handling the big tree trunks, some of which weighed a few tons. You had to be careful, because if one of those fell on you there would be no second chance. Werner's business involved moving and storing the trunks. There was another company, which organised the chopping down of the trees high up on the hillside. Werner had a lorry, which brought the trunks down to the compound from the cutting areas. Including Franz, he had three employees.

Franz was soon able to do the work. He was always good with his hands. All four workers were expected to be able to do every aspect of the job, so within a month Franz could do it all. He learnt how to drive the truck and the lorry, which he enjoyed the most. It was very cold in January and February 1949. Sometimes work had to stop for two or three days when the track up the hillside was blocked by snow.

Werner's other two employees were similar in age to Franz. One of them lived at home with his parents, but the other, like Franz, had a room in the village. They were all single. They went out together several times a week in the evening, usually to one of the two pubs on the main square.

Franz decided he had better write to his mother, Eva, in Kornwestheim to let her know where he was. She wrote back to say that she and Josef were still living in the camp. Josef was behaving strangely. They had been arguing a lot, and he kept calling her a witch. She had asked to be moved out of the camp, but the council always seemed to find other people who were more in need. It wasn't as crowded now in the camp, and the huts had been partitioned so that they had a room of their own, with a sink and a stove with a small, two-ring, electric cooker, but it was still a camp.

Franz had a succession of girlfriends. He found that they liked to hear him talk. That was one thing he was very good at. In fact, once he got started he soon lost all track of time. He could go on for hours on end. The trouble was that, like most eighteen-year-old boys, he wanted to try out sex. Unfortunately, the girls he went out with were only interested in marriage. He wasn't ready for that.

He worked in Niederalm through 1949. He enjoyed the work, but was becoming a little bored with following the same daily routines, and seeing the same friends when he wasn't at work.

In December he had a very lucky escape. He was

driving the lorry back down the hill to the compound with a full load of trunks. In fact the lorry was overloaded, and the load hadn't been properly secured. As he took a bend on a steep section of the track where he was forced to brake, part of the load broke loose. Several trunks slid forwards, smashed through the back of the cab and into the windscreen. One of them scraped his arm and pushed him sideways into the cab door. If that had been a few inches further to the left it would have smashed him into the windscreen. He was shaken, but, apart from a bruised right arm, he was unhurt. For the third time in his life he was lucky to escape serious injury or death.

In January 1950 there was a very heavy snowfall that continued without pause for two days. The chopping of trees was forced to stop, and in any case the lorry couldn't get up the track to bring them down. Within a week all the stocks in the compound had gone and they had no work. There was a further heavy snowfall, and there was no chance of any logging work re-starting for at least another two weeks. Franz decided that this was an omen, telling him it was time to move on. He was becoming bored with Niederalm in any case.

He told Werner that he wanted to go see his parents, and thought that now would be as good a time as any for him to make the trip. Werner asked him if he would be coming back.

"I am not sure," replied Franz. "It depends what the situation is in Kornwestheim. If I don't get back here by 1st March I guess you can say I'm not coming."

Franz said his farewells, packed his few things and left Niederalm.

By this time the flood of refugees from the east into Germany had slowed to a trickle, though it never stopped completely. From now on it was people wanting to get away from the harsh Communist regimes ruling all the Eastern European countries. With the exception of Tito's Jugoslavia, these regimes carried out Russian policies, which were strictly enforced with the help of secret police forces. Many people were prepared to leave their countries of birth to face the uncertainties of new lives in the free states of the West. Providing they could prove reasonably a German background, no matter how long it had been since their ancestors had left Germany, they were accepted into the FDR, the new West German State.

Most of those crossing the borders at the major checkpoints had the correct documents, so there were few problems. Franz caught the train from Salzburg to Munich, then another to Stuttgart, from where a local train took him to Kornwestheim.

As the train approached the station he could see that there had been plenty of new building going on in the town. Not all of it was new housing for refugees. There were new road signs pointing to places with English names. Large permanent blocks were being built in the town, but also just outside. The greater Stuttgart area was designated for the American occupying troops. Some of these out-of-town barracks were as big as a village, or a small town, and they had all the amenities to enable their occupants to live completely independently of the local population. Franz didn't know it then, but these barracks were to be occupied by American forces for more than forty years.

He made his way to the camp where his mother and father still lived. Josef hadn't got a permanent job. He occasionally found work on one of the building sites, but he was often ill and not capable of going to work. Employers would avoid taking on someone they knew to be unreliable unless they were really desperate. Eva had got a job working in a factory helping to prepare dinners in the canteen.

She began to realise that her marriage was falling apart. The arguments were happening nearly every day, and Josef kept calling her a witch. She suspected that he had a woman friend in the town. Since Josef worked on an occasional basis she didn't know where he spent his time when she was at work. The enforced "no sex" rule between the couple didn't help matters.

Franz was able to stay with his parents in the camp. He spent a week looking for jobs, which might be permanent, rather than temporary. All he was offered were a few hours' work here and there. He didn't want that.

He saw that his mother and father were unhappy. His father suffered from big swings of mood change. Sometimes he was fine, but, for no reason, he would pick an argument with Eva, and with Franz. Josef was a big man. He had recovered his physical strength, but Franz had grown, and he was fit and strong. He would not receive any more of the beatings his father had inflicted on him back on the farm in Elek.

After two weeks Franz knew that he couldn't carry on living with his parents. He went to the council employment office to see what they thought about job prospects.

"The job situation is going to stay bad for some time in the south of Germany," said the clerk. "There are far more refugees than we can find work for. It will improve, but it will take time. Why don't you go up to the Ruhr? They need workers in the steel foundries and the mines. A lot of the workforce was killed in the war, and they haven't had sufficient numbers of refugees to take their places. You will get a job up there."

Franz weighed up the possibilities. Foundries and mines, not the sort of work he thought he would like, and he had no experience. He had been through a lot in the last five years, more than many people experience in a lifetime. Maybe this was something else he had to go through in order to find out what he was going to do with his life.

He packed up, said his goodbyes, and caught a train north to Frankfurt.

From there he took another train which took him to Essen in the heart of the industrial Ruhr. The whole area seemed to Franz to consist of smoking chimneys, dirty factories, and coal spoil heaps. Having come from a small village in the middle of the largest farming area of Hungary, he had never imagined the existence of somewhere like this.

But one of Franz's attributes was his ability to adapt, and he was always willing to try something new. So he had soon found a room to stay in overnight, and the following day he went to the employment office to look for work.

The immediate response was that there was no call for farm workers or people with logging experience in that area. Most of the factories wanted people with some relevant training, and he had none. That left the mines, where there was more demand for labourers. They would also train those who wanted to learn.

There were immediate vacancies in a mine near the town of Bochum, about ten miles to the east of Essen.

Franz took the details given to him at the employment office and made his way to Bochum and the mine. The mine was short of workers and he was taken on immediately.

He found a room in the town and soon settled into a routine. He was given training for one week, and then found himself working at the coalface. The work was hard and very dirty, but there was a camaraderie amongst the miners, and the money was good. Demand for the coal was such that for much of the time they worked a full six days every week. They would probably have worked all seven days, but there had to be one day a week where the engineers worked on the shafts and equipment, making sure they were kept operational and as safe as possible for the workers.

The hard work meant that Franz was very tired most of the time, and he had virtually no social life.

Towards the end of August 1951, after he had been in Bochum for well over a year, he got a letter from his mother saying that Josef had applied for a divorce.

Eva, having been brought up as a staunch Catholic, didn't believe in divorce, but she knew she couldn't carry on living with Josef. He had now been diagnosed as schizophrenic. On one occasion she had lit the fire in the stove only to find that the smoke was coming back into the room instead of going up the chimney. When she looked she found that clothes had been pushed up the chimney to block it. After she had cleaned up the mess and Josef had returned home, she asked him why he had blocked the chimney.

"You are a witch," shouted Josef. "If you can't have a fire for the stove you can't brew your potions to poison me."

On another occasion she saw Josef leaving home carrying some clean bed sheets. She followed him to the house of his woman friend. It was now open knowledge that he had a married woman as a girlfriend. Josef went into the house and came out a short time later without the sheets. Eva kept out of his sight, but then went straight to the police station. A policeman was sent with Eva to the woman's house, and the woman had to give back the sheets to Eva.

As Franz read about these events in his mother's letter he knew she was right. Whether they divorced or not was irrelevant. They could not go on living together.

Franz decided it was time to leave the Ruhr. He knew he didn't want to be a miner all his life.

At the end of September he moved back to Kornwestheim. His parents had finally left the camp and moved into a small flat, so he moved in with them. The divorce was in progress, and would soon be finalised. His mother was already looking for somewhere else to live.

Franz went to the employment office to look for work. Prospects had improved considerably since he had left for the Ruhr. He was offered a job in an engineering factory to train as a fitter. He decided it would be a good idea to learn a trade. There were a lot of farms in this area of Baden-Württemberg, and many vineyards in the Neckar valley, just to the east of Kornwestheim, but none of them were advertising for workers, and he wasn't sure if he wanted to go back to working on the land. He decided to take the job and train to be a fitter.

It was impossible for Eva to find another flat, so she went to the council offices for help. The council was still forcing local people with spare rooms to accommodate refugees. The council found a small house for Eva and Franz in a quiet street on the south side of Kornwestheim, not far from the centre. They could have the upper floor. The widow who owned the house was disgusted at being forced to provide them with a room. She made Eva sign a form to say that they would have no visitors, and no children were to be brought to the house.

Eva and Franz left Josef in the flat and moved to live at the woman's house. By the end of 1951 the divorce was finalised. Although there had been little love in the marriage at any time Eva had been brought up as a staunch Catholic. They may have been legally divorced, but so far as she was concerned they would always be married in the eyes of God.

Franz and his mother settled into the new routine. Eva took after her father in one respect. She could look after money. Her family had worked hard in Hungary to develop their business as landowners, and despite the Hungarian inheritance laws they had managed to keep their wealth until most of it was taken from them at the end of the Second World War. Eva was determined to have a home of her own again before she died, and she worked hard to save as much as she could. As she worked in a canteen she was able to bring home left-over food, and they saved considerably on eating costs. She couldn't expect any help from her parents in Hungary, so she would have to do it all by herself.

Unfortunately Franz took after his father's side of the family. He couldn't look after money at all. As soon as it was earned it was spent.

Franz wanted girlfriends, but he didn't have much success. His workplace was almost totally a male preserve. He just didn't seem to be able to find a girl.

He confided in one of his work mates.

"I think there must be something wrong with me. I just don't get to meet any girls."

"You need to go where the unattached girls are. Have you tried going to dances?"

"I can't dance," said Franz.

"Well it's time for you to learn, maybe."

"Yes, but where?" thought Franz to himself.

He looked on the staff notice board in the canteen. He had seen dances advertised there before. In the bottom corner someone had pinned a handwritten notice:

> "Individual dancing tuition offered at very reasonable rates.—Apply Fr. Muller, packing department."

When he went down to the packing department he was surprised to find that Frau Muller was a young woman of about eighteen.

"Do you teach dancing?"

She told him that she could teach him the basic steps for most of the modern dances. Her name was Erika, she lived with her parents, and the house had a room big enough for just a small number of people to be taught at a time. It had a wooden floor. She had a wind-up gramophone and a few records.

They arranged to meet at her home the following Sunday afternoon.

Franz soon realised that he would never be the smoothest mover on a dance floor, but that wasn't why he was taking lessons. He just wanted to know he wouldn't make a complete fool of himself. He arranged to take lessons every Sunday afternoon. Sometimes he was the only student, but occasionally another younger boy came to the sessions.

On the first Sunday in March 1953 he went for his fourth lesson. This time there was another girl with Erika, of similar age to her. She was fairly tall, attractive, with medium-length black hair, and smartly dressed.

"This is my friend, Victoria Moser. She has come over for the day from Karlsruhe."

Franz had his lesson as usual, but he wasn't doing very well. Victoria laughed when he got it wrong and he was tripping over his own feet. That didn't help his confidence. After half an hour he had had enough.

"I just can't get it together today," he said. "I think I will go to the café for a coffee." As an afterthought he added, "Would you both like to come?"

Erika said she couldn't. She had another lesson in half an hour.

"Why don't you go, Victoria?"

Victoria agreed. She would have to wait for another hour before her friend was free, and she quite liked the look of Franz.

So they went for traditional German Sunday afternoon "coffee and cake".

They talked easily together. They compared notes about their Hungarian backgrounds. Victoria thought she had never heard a man talk so much. He certainly had few inhibitions. The time passed quickly and he took her back to Erika's.

As he was about to leave her at the front door he asked her, "Will you be visiting again soon?"

"Probably," she replied. "I think there is a dance in two weeks on the Saturday night."

"Maybe I'll see you there," said Franz, and set off home.

Victoria came to Kornwestheim for the dance. She went with Erika. Franz was there and they met each other. He asked her to dance. He still wasn't much good at it, and he was glad when it ended. They got a drink and found somewhere away from the band to sit down. They carried on the conversation where they had left off two weeks earlier. They lost track of time and didn't have another dance that evening.

Victoria was surprised when Erika came to tell her it was time to go home.

"Are you staying over tonight?" asked Franz.

"Yes, I'm staying with Erika."

"Would you like to go for a walk tomorrow morning?"

"Why not?" replied Victoria. "But I have to catch the eleven-thirty a.m. train back to Karlsruhe."

They met the next morning near the centre of town. They walked past the big shoe factory and out on a path between fields into the country. It was dry but very cold. They talked constantly and didn't really notice the cold.

Victoria realised it was nearly time to catch her train.

"When will you come again?" asked Franz.

Victoria couldn't stop herself.

"I'll ask Erika if I can stay with her at Whitsuntide for a couple of days. You can check with her if you like."

Franz took Victoria to the station. The train arrived. As she was about to get on she turned to say goodbye, but instead they kissed briefly. Then she was gone.

Whitsuntide was at the end of May that year. Franz kept up his dancing lessons with Erika, though he didn't improve much.

Two weeks before Whitsuntide Erika told him that Victoria was coming for the weekend.

He arranged to come to meet her at Erika's.

They spent most of the weekend together. Franz took Victoria to the flat and introduced her to Eva. By the end of Whitsunday there wasn't much they didn't know about each other's backgrounds.

Victoria told him that she knew that her oldest brother Peter had reverted to his old ways. Even though he was married to Inge and they had a young son, he had at least two other girlfriends in Karlsruhe. He would never change. She thought that Inge probably knew about the other women, but she didn't seem to want to do anything about it. As for her other brother Reiner, it didn't look as if he would ever get married. At least the family would soon be able to move out of the nasty woman's house. They were going to live in two rooms in a row of wooden terraces that were almost finished.

Franz said that he didn't like his new landlady. The rules

of the house were very strict. He hadn't seen his father since the divorce.

On Whit Monday they walked again in the fields. Victoria wanted to catch the six p.m. train back home. After lunch Eva said she was going to see a work colleague in Stuttgart, and would probably not be back until after Victoria had left.

After Eva had gone, Franz said, "Do you want to go out again now?"

"No," said Victoria. "I've had enough walking for today. Besides it looks like rain."

Suddenly, out of the blue, he asked, "Have you ever had sex?"

Victoria was taken aback.

"No. It's too risky. I can't afford to have a baby."

"It's not so risky. The chances of getting pregnant the first time are very small."

Victoria was rather naïve and somewhat ignorant in the matter of conception.

Now he had broached the matter, Franz carried on talking, trying to persuade her. He would take precautions so she wouldn't get pregnant.

After a few minutes she was starting to waver. There was an opportunity now which might not occur again for a long time.

Finally she agreed, and they made love in Franz's bed. He didn't use a contraceptive. He had never had any intention of doing so. He had a notion that he wanted to see if he could father a child.

Victoria felt very bad about it afterwards, but it was too late now. She had done it.

Franz was pleased with himself.

They said little for the rest of the afternoon, in fact right up to their kissing goodbye when she caught her train.

"I'll see you soon," shouted Franz as the train pulled out of the station.

Victoria didn't visit Kornwestheim again for several weeks. She wrote to tell Franz she would be coming, and he met her at the station. She looked apprehensive as she got off the train.

"Shall we go to the flat?"

"No." said Victoria. "Let's go for a coffee first."

They settled down in the corner of the café with their drinks.

"What's the problem?" asked Franz.

"I think I'm pregnant."

Victoria was indeed pregnant, though it was another two weeks before it was confirmed. Of course Eva had to be told, as well as Anna, Peter and Reiner.

Peter decided that it was all Franz's fault, and as Victoria's eldest brother he would go to tell Franz what he thought of him.

He duly turned up at the flat and Franz showed him in. Peter put on his "big brother" act. He started to remonstrate with Franz for making his sister pregnant.

Franz wasn't prepared to take this from Peter.

"From what I hear you have been up to a few tricks of your own since you got married, so who are you to tell me off?"

This took Peter aback, and he started to fluster.

"Look, I know it's natural for a man to be after sex,

but you have to be careful the girl doesn't get pregnant, and you have to keep quiet about it."

As far as Franz was concerned this was as good as a confession from Peter. Peter never tried the "big brother" act with Franz again.

There were few situations of greater disgrace than being an unmarried mother. It was not something either family would tolerate, particularly the two mothers.

Franz went to Karlsruhe to meet the rest of Victoria's family. They had just moved into a two-roomed flat in a row of wooden terraces. It was late July 1953.

Victoria and Franz went for a walk to be able to talk alone.

"Have you thought about getting an abortion?" said Franz.

Victoria gasped. Abortions were illegal and dangerous.

"I am not going to take such a risk. Besides how would we be able to find someone to do it, anyone we dare trust? Definitely not."

"Well, I suppose we had better fix a wedding date," said Franz.

Victoria knew that if she became a single mother she would be regarded as a slut, and the families would not stand for the disgrace. She could see that Franz did not want to get married, but there was no alternative for either of them.

Once that had been agreed Anna and the brothers could be told, and a start could be made on arrangements for the wedding. Eva had already said that Victoria could move into the flat she shared with Franz. Eva would find somewhere else to live. Victoria didn't want to leave her family in Karlsruhe, or her job as a maid, until she had to.

The wedding was fixed for the last Friday in August, at the registry office in the town hall in Kornwestheim. It was to be a very low-key affair. Victoria would not be dressed in white.

On the big day Victoria, Anna, Reiner, Peter, Inge and their son, now five years old, caught the train to Kornwestheim. They went to the flat where Eva and Franz lived.

They all walked to the registry office for the ceremony which was scheduled for two-thirty p.m.

The only other person to join the family group was Erika. Franz's father, Josef, had been told about the marriage, but he didn't turn up. The simple ceremony was soon over. Everyone went back to the flat for food and drinks. At last people started to relax, and for a couple of hours it became a jolly party.

The time came for Anna and her family to catch the train back to Karlsruhe. Victoria said goodbye to Franz and left with her mother. There wasn't going to be a honeymoon.

For the next few months Victoria and Franz lived separately. It wasn't until Christmas time that Victoria moved to Kornwestheim. Eva had recently moved out of the flat into another room she had found nearby. The landlady had been told that Victoria was moving in. She didn't like the idea, but there wasn't anything she could do about it. Victoria had left her job in Karlsruhe, and there wasn't much point in her trying to find work before the baby was due. Franz was out at work for most of the day, so Victoria did the shopping, cooking, and cleaned the flat.

She soon found her way around Kornwestheim. It was small enough for everywhere in the town to be reached on foot.

The landlady didn't realise at first that Victoria was pregnant. It wasn't until after Christmas 1953 that the "bump" became obvious. Once she realised what was about to happen, the landlady confronted Franz and Victoria.

"You can't have a child here. You signed the agreement. You will have to move out before the child is born."

They did try to find another flat where a baby would be accepted, but didn't have any success. Accommodation of any kind was still very hard to find.

By the middle of January 1954 Victoria was getting to be quite big. The steep stairs to the first floor room were becoming hard work. The baby was due at the end of February. Victoria was surprised when very early in the morning of 5th February things started to happen. The waters broke. Victoria tried to wake Franz. He was fast asleep and didn't like being wakened. At first he wouldn't accept that the baby was on the way. She finally managed to get him out of bed and sent him to phone for a taxi.

Franz went with Victoria to the hospital in Ludwigsburg. He had to wait in a corridor near to the delivery room. He had been chain smoking almost non-stop since they left the flat.

A nurse gave Victoria a quick examination, and she was taken straight into the delivery room. She didn't have to wait long.

In February 1954, Victoria, who was now twenty years

old, gave birth to a healthy baby girl. Despite the fact that the baby arrived more than three weeks sooner than expected, she was of average birth weight.

Franz and Victoria hadn't discussed a possible name for the baby much. The following day, when Victoria had recovered a little from the birth, they discussed a name in more detail.

They both thought they would like a name to remind them of their Hungarian origins, but they didn't want to follow the old custom of taking a name from a close relative. They wanted something a little unusual, a name which people would be likely to remember. After a lot of discussion they agreed to call their daughter Marika.

It was a week before Victoria and Marika could go home from the hospital. Anna had arrived at the flat to stay with Victoria for a few days to help with the baby. Anna got the message to collect Victoria from the hospital. She ordered a taxi and went for her daughter and grand-daughter. They were soon back at the flat. Their arrival home wasn't the happy event it should have been, because the landlady confronted them at the entrance door to the building.

"You can't keep the baby here. I won't allow it. The flat is too small anyway."

They didn't argue with her, but went up to the flat. Victoria had more to worry about than the landlady's objections. She had to care for her baby.

A short time later Franz arrived. He was angry and shouted at Anna and Victoria.

"I have just been by taxi to the hospital and back. Why didn't you let me know you had gone?"

Anna said, "I didn't know that they had told you too. What kind of welcome is that for your new baby?"

Franz was still seething, but gradually calmed down.

The landlady went to the council offices to try to get some advice. She wanted to know how she could enforce the rental agreement and have the family evicted.

The official didn't hold out any hope for her.

"You will find it impossible to enforce the agreement. No judge will let you throw out a mother with a baby in the current housing shortage."

The landlady went to confront Franz and Eva once more with what the official had told her. She hoped that Franz, Victoria and the baby would find somewhere else to live. Franz just shrugged his shoulders. He wasn't going to move unless he was forced to.

The landlady wasn't happy, but she couldn't alter the situation. That didn't mean she was going to be pleasant to the family. They had better keep the baby quiet.

Franz bought a pram for the baby. This was a big, heavy pram.

There was no hallway in the flats downstairs, and it wasn't possible to leave the pram outside on the pavement. When Franz wasn't there, Victoria had to struggle to drag this pram up and down the stairs, to and from the flat.

Marika turned out to be a quiet child, and there was little the landlady could complain about, though that didn't stop her moaning at Victoria whenever they bumped into each other.

Franz adopted a strange attitude to the baby at first. He ignored Marika as much as he could. He had no feelings for this child. She was the cause of his situation. His freedom had been taken away because of her. He felt he was now trapped forever in a marriage he didn't want. Somehow it was all the fault of the baby and none of his own.

He wanted Victoria to put the baby in a day nursery and get a job.

Victoria refused. "I am going to stay at home to look after Marika, at least until she is two years old. Then we will see."

Franz began to mellow a little only when Marika began to walk and talk.

So for the first two years of her life Marika lived with her parents in an upstairs room near to the centre of Kornwestheim.

# Chapter Nine

BY 1950, THE influx of refugees from the east into Germany had slowed to a trickle. The Iron Curtain was firmly drawn, and the borders were strictly controlled. Stalin died in 1953, but it was some years before there was any noticeable softening in Russian policy. Every new regime had to establish its total control before it could consider any changes in policy.

Throughout the early and mid-1950s the West German authorities were trying to improve housing conditions, especially for the refugees, many of who were living in temporary accommodation or were still in other residents' houses. The ruins of wartime had finally been cleared and building for the future was well under way. In Stuttgart, thousands of tons of rubble had been dumped on one site to the north of the city centre, creating a mountain of rubble. The council decided to level it and cover it with soil. Subsequently a large commercial exhibition centre was built on the site. You could say that the new Germany was being built over the ruins of the old.

In 1956, Anna and Reiner Moser were moved out of the wooden terrace block they had gone to at the time

Victoria got married. New terrace blocks had been built at the edge of the fields around Karlsruhe. They were very similar in design to the temporary wooden terraces, but they were built of brick, with tiled roofs.

Within these blocks, groups of four flats were built around a central passage, two upstairs and two down. Each pair of flats had to share a toilet. There were two rooms in each flat, a combined living/dining room/kitchen, and a bedroom. There was no bathroom. Anna and Reiner moved into one of these ground-floor flats.

Anna continued to suffer from nightmares, and from panic attacks at other times too. She became paranoid about anyone who knocked at the door of the flat, fearing that it was the police coming to take her away. She had never liked going to see a doctor, believing that if she had a medical problem it would cure itself with time. Niggling pains she just put down to her getting older. Reiner became very worried about her, and finally managed to convince her to go to the doctor. She was referred to the psychiatric department at the local hospital. It was decided she should undergo a course of electric shock treatment, which was considered at the time helpful for patients suffering from mental problems. From the patient's point of view such treatment was extremely painful and traumatic. Powerful electric shocks were fired directly into the brain. After the treatments Anna didn't seem to have any more attacks. Whether the treatment cured the problem, or whether the fear of having to undergo more of the same treatment caused Anna to control the outward symptoms is open to conjecture. In any case Anna didn't complain of more attacks, so it appears that the treatment achieved its purpose. Any other of her ailments she continued to suffer in silence.

There was building work going on round the outskirts of Kornwestheim too. This was specifically designated for refugees, and Franz put the family's name on the waiting list. He was told that priority was being given to families with four or more people. He spoke to Eva. She wasn't keen on the idea of living with her son and his wife and baby, but she agreed, so that the family could move out of their upstairs flat and away from their unpleasant landlady.

They were allocated a flat in one of the last blocks to be completed. The blocks were substantial three-storey buildings. There were a number of sections of flats per block, each with its own entrance door. Each section had three flats on each floor, with doors leading off a central staircase. The entrance door of each flat opened into a small hallway, with a door leading off at the side into the combined toilet and bathroom. There wasn't enough space for a full-sized bath. When taking a bath you had to sit, you couldn't lie down. In the bathroom was a coal-burning boiler for heating water. This was lit only on Saturdays in order to provide hot water for a weekly bath, and to do the washing.

The door at the end of the hallway opened into the living room. This wasn't very big, about twelve feet square. A curtain in one corner led to a very small kitchen, which had a gas cooker, and at the opposite corner of the living room doors led off to two bedrooms, one about twice the size of the other. There was a large basement, divided into sections by wooden partitions, so that each flat in the building had its own storage area. The blocks were well built, and properly insulated, both in the construction of the walls, and by deep double-glazed windows. There was further protection against the weather by means of substantial wooden shutters hung on the outside of the windows. Only the living room was heated, by means of a coal-burning stove at one side. There were open spaces between the blocks of flats, where residents could hang out their washing, or sit out on the grass in summer.

Franz and the family were put in the last block, so that the view from their front window was of allotments, rather than of another block of flats. This wasn't going to change. The land to the east was a collecting area for the town water supply, and further building on it was prohibited.

They were put in a flat in the middle floor, with flats directly above and below theirs. Marika was two years old when they moved in. Eva slept in the small bedroom, Franz, Victoria and Marika in the large one.

Victoria never grew to like Eva. She didn't seem to have a loving or friendly side to her nature. She didn't display any warmth of feeling to the baby, or even to her own son. Franz was more affectionate, taking after his father's family, rather than his mother. Unlike his mother, he was likely to take spur-of-the-moment decisions without thinking through the likely consequences. Detailed planning, medium or long-term was not in his make-up. Eva was more cool, calculating and businesslike, taking after her father.

They didn't cook or eat together. Eva ate mostly at the canteen where she worked, and lived her own life, which revolved around her work. She spent little of her earnings, saving as much as possible.

Victoria knew that the time was coming when she would have to find work. The biggest employer in the town was the shoe factory, which was one of the largest in Germany, so she went to enquire there. She was in luck. They were looking for more workers, and would take her on. There was one problem. Who was going to look after Marika? Victoria tried to find nursery accommodation, but there were no places, and there were long waiting lists. The shoe factory had set up its own kindergarten, but could only take children over the age of four. Victoria didn't want to lose the job she had been offered. She wrote to her mother, Anna, in Karlsruhe. Could she look after Marika until nursery accommodation became available?

Anna was delighted to help. Franz and Victoria took Marika to Karlsruhe to stay with Anna and Reiner in their new flat. Marika wasn't upset at having to leave her mother and stay with her grandmother. Anna had a loving and affectionate nature, totally different from Eva. She enjoyed having Marika there, and made a fuss of her. Reiner wasn't too pleased at first at having a toddler in the flat, but Marika showed him a lot of affection, and he soon mellowed.

Franz and Victoria began to enjoy life more. They both enjoyed going to the cinema, and popular music. They visited Marika in Karlsruhe about once every six weeks.

ઈ

Events in their native Hungary took a dramatic turn for the worse. Soviet leader Khruschev had turned against the policies of Stalin. The government in Hungary saw this as an opportunity for reform against strict Communist ideals. The Soviet regime couldn't allow the reforms, and removed popular premier Imre Nagy. The population of Budapest took to the streets in open revolt. On 4th November 1956, Soviet troops with tanks entered Budapest to put down the revolt by force. The rest of the world looked on aghast, but there was nobody with the strength to act against the power of the Soviets. Nagy was to be held a prisoner for over eighteen months before suffering a secret trial and execution.

The powers of both Eastern and Western blocks were developing and openly testing the hydrogen bomb. There was potential for conflict between the two main political ideologies at many flashpoints around the world. These were dangerous times, and anyone in the world with access to the news media knew it. They also knew that there was nothing they could do to alter the situation individually. Various organisations sprang up, in Western Europe in particular, in order to protest against the testing and stockpiling of nuclear weapons. Although they gained a great deal of media coverage the affect on the nuclear powers was very limited.

ॐ

Franz hadn't lost his independent streak. He didn't like anyone telling him what he should do. He didn't help around the flat. Victoria had to do all the cleaning and cooking, even though she was now working full-time. Franz would take decisions without consulting Victoria, which caused rows. He was not good with the finances, but wouldn't allow Victoria to take control of them. One day he arrived home from work and announced to Victoria that he had bought a car.

"What do you mean, you've bought a car? What with?"

"Two hundred marks down, and the rest over three years."

Victoria made Franz show her the loan agreement. It registered with her very quickly what he had done.

She screamed at him. "The monthly payment is almost as much as the amount you earn. That means we will have to live on what I earn until it is paid for. You are mad!"

The argument went on for some time, but it made no difference. The deed was done.

At least from then on they didn't have to visit Karlsruhe by train.

Marika spent most of her time in the late 1950s with Anna and Reiner in Karlsruhe. She became friendly with other young children living nearby. There were lots of places to play that were safe for the children. Anna got an allotment, where she grew vegetables and fruit. It reminded her of her days in Nagymányok where the family had grown much of their own food. Marika helped herself to whatever was ripe, and Anna didn't stop her. Once Marika ate so many tomatoes that she was sick. Another time it was peaches. For years afterwards she couldn't face eating tomatoes or peaches.

Sometimes Peter, Inge and their son Andras would visit. Anna had become considerably overweight. When she laughed her whole body shook, and the fat round her tummy wobbled. Andras begged her to laugh so he could watch her wobbling tummy.

Once Andras had started school, Inge got a job as a

waitress in the canteen of the local council finance office. She worked part-time, so that she could be home when Andras came in from school. Peter had been working as a locksmith, which he hated. He much preferred driving for the Americans, when he got the chance. A girlfriend of Inge's had married an American soldier, so they became friendly with a few Americans, and often had parties with American guests. Andras didn't like these parties, or the Americans.

Inge found out about a vacancy for a driver who was needed to act as a chauffeur for senior council officials. Peter applied for and got the job. He was delighted with the prospect. The work was easy. There were long periods of inactivity between the actual driving, which he didn't mind at all. He would deliver an official to a destination, and be told to collect him two or three hours later. In the waiting time he could do what he wanted. He couldn't have wished for a more suitable job.

The black market didn't disappear completely for a number of years. Peter had continued to make money by using his American contacts, selling things they could provide to the German population. These were goods, which were still only available on ration, or simply unobtainable in Germany at the time. Peter and his family accumulated quite a lot of money, but they were careful not to display their wealth too much, because the legality of its sources was questionable, and the less anyone had a reason to pry the better.

Reiner had occasional girlfriends, but showed no sign of wanting to marry. He became friendly with a young woman, who worked as a hairdresser. She was married with a young child, but her Italian husband had gone back to Italy, and didn't appear to want to come back to her. It looked as if the relationship between Reiner and this woman would develop into something more permanent.

The woman saved enough money to open her own hairdressing business. She soon had staff working for her and became quite successful. Reiner had been dithering in making any firm decision regarding the relationship. He was looking for someone who could be a good cook and housekeeper. In the end the decision was taken out of his hands. The husband in Italy had found out that his wife had started her own successful business, and he decided to return to her.

When Marika was four, in 1958, she could go to the kindergarten run by the shoe factory in Kornwestheim. Victoria took her there. Marika didn't know any of the staff, or the other children. As her mother left her on the first morning she stood pressed against the window with tears streaming down her face. In the years before she started school she was never happy there.

She was frequently ill with the usual childhood illnesses, such as measles and mumps. Whenever she became ill her father would take her to Anna's in Karlsruhe. Once there she would stay for six weeks or so until her parents came to take her back to Kornwestheim. In later years she went there for the school holidays in any case. In effect she spent most of her early childhood at her grandmother's in Karlsruhe, from the age of two until she went to school at the age of seven in 1961.

The kindergarten was run more as a crèche. It took the children of employees until they were old enough to be at home alone. That meant that there was a range of children from the ages of four to about twelve years old. When school had finished each day at one o' clock, the children went straight to the kindergarten. There they were given lunch which was sent down from the canteen in the shoe factory. They stayed in the kindergarten until it was time to meet their mothers when they finished work at four o' clock.

The older children were given more creative things to do. At Christmas they would present a show in front of the workers in the factory. In the kindergarten they could play the latest popular music, which the children could dance to. Sometimes a salesman would come from the factory asking for children with specific shoe sizes. They would go up to the factory to model shoes in front of visiting buyers.

By the beginning of the 'sixties Marika was spending most of her time in Kornwestheim. She was glad that her grandmother, Eva, no longer lived with the family. Eva had moved out into a flat of her own in 1958, once the family knew there was no danger of Franz and Victoria losing their flat. Germany was now making big progress economically. The foreign aid after the war had helped, and it was somewhat better to build from the base of total wartime devastation. It's often easier to start from nothing than to repair and modernise damaged properties and broken machines. Building "new" meant the latest model of machine or the latest ideas in buildings design, and Germany was gaining an economic advantage over the rest of the European countries trying to re-build their economies after the war.

There was still contact with relatives in Hungary. The families had always exchanged cards at Christmas. It gradually became easier for visits to be made in both directions. Eva had made a trip to Elek to see her parents before her father died in 1959. Eva visited two or three families fairly regularly in Kornwestheim who had come from Hungary. The train, which had brought Josef, Eva and Franz Sellner to Ludwigsburg after the war had carried many people from the Elek area, and several had settled in Kornwestheim.

Maria Nagy came to visit from Kismányok. She continued to live with her husband, Hartmut, and his parents at the farmhouse in Kismányok. They had two children, a boy and a girl. The house was crowded, and a very unhappy place to live. Hartmut's father was a violent brute. He made everyone's life a misery, particularly his wife's.

As the German economy became stronger, the government passed laws to make compensation payments to those Germans who had been dispossessed of their properties in those countries now under Communist rule. Eva went to see Josef to ask if he was going to put in a claim for the farm in Hungary. He wasn't interested in receiving any money for the farm. Eva told him that she would claim, and if he didn't want any of the proceeds she would keep all the money. Her parents were now dead, and her brother and sister-in-law had perished in the Russian labour camps after the War. Eva claimed for her parents' and her brothers' land, and obtained payments for both in addition to that for the farm. She put this money in her existing savings account, to which she added regularly from her small earnings, with the intention that she would eventually be able to buy a house. Her father's business acumen still ran through her brain. It was a pity that Franz took more after his father's family in financial skills.

All the families in the flats where Franz and his family lived had been refugees. They had come from various countries in the east, or from East Germany. Most were of similar ages to Franz and Victoria. They all had children, so the kids played out together.

The immediate neighbours had a daughter of Marika's age, so they played together most days. Marika never had many toys. There never seemed to be enough money for such things in the household. Her neighbour always had a lot of nice toys, so she was happy to play with her.

Franz sometimes arranged little parties in the flat with the neighbours next door, and perhaps one or two others in the building. They would drink beer. They made a little space so that they could dance to music on the record player. One of their favourites at the time was the twist, partly because they didn't need much space for that.

This was a happy time for the family. They were often short of money, but still could enjoy themselves a little. Only once in this period did the family go away for a holiday together. Franz borrowed a tent, and drove north to Blankenberge, on the coast of Belgium, where they camped for a week.

❧

The political turmoil going on in Hungary in the mid and late 'fifties, culminating in the uprising and invasion by Russian forces early in November 1956, had little direct effect on the remoter rural areas, such as Elek and Kismányok. Of course everyone heard the reports of the troubles, and for some time afterwards there was visible evidence of more troops and police, but families who worked the land for seven days a week in order to survive had little time to get involved with politics. The Russians installed Janos Kadar as Prime Minister. There was a very harsh crackdown on all dissidents, real or imagined, in order to re-establish the Communist regime. It was always apparent in Hungary that the Communists never had majority popular support, but Kadar stayed in power for over thirty years. Over that period the regime very gradually became less oppressive, as it did in several of the European Communist states. Most of the people remained poor. They suffered Communism, because they had no choice.

By the end of the 'fifties Communism as a creed had spread around the globe, often to some unexpected places. After the Cuban revolution had succeeded in changing the government at the beginning of 1959, Castro had set up a Soviet-backed regime right under America's nose, and almost within sight of its borders. Despite the murder and oppression of opponents by Communist regimes, many otherwise sensible people proposed Communism as the political system to follow. After all, didn't capitalism kill people so that the privileged few could obtain and keep all the wealth?

As always, you can fool most of the people all of the time.

## Chapter Ten

1961 SAW THE physical division of Berlin by the building of the Wall.

As it was being built, at the age of seven, Marika started at her first school. There was a tradition for children to be made a fuss of on their first day. Victoria bought a huge cardboard cone, specially made for the purpose, and available in local shops at the start of each new school year. This she filled with sweets. Marika had her photo taken on the main steps at the front of the school holding the cone, which was almost as big as she was. The school was less than ten minutes' walk away from home, not far from the parish church in the old part of Kornwestheim. Marika soon grew to enjoy school, and made good progress.

The military powers of America and Russia squared up to each other in October 1962 in what was to be their major military confrontation of the Cold War. High-flying aircraft from the USA had photographed missile bases being developed in Cuba. American President Kennedy demanded the removal of the bases. Russian leader Khruschev refused to bow to American demands. The Americans surrounded Cuba with a naval blockade preventing Russian ships from delivering supplies. For more than a week the world held its breath. In the end Khruschev backed down, and the bases were dismantled.

Major events may be taking place in the world, but at best ordinary people can do no more than watch the news, and get on with their lives.

Reiner would be thirty-nine years old late in 1962. He had a new girlfriend. She and her sister shared a flat in Karlsruhe, near the city centre. They were from the Pfalz region, a little to the north of Karlsruhe, and had moved to the city for their work. Their father was a clergyman, who had married three times, following the deaths of each of his first two wives. There were children in each marriage, and it was a big family, so home was pretty crowded.

Reiner's relationship with one sister didn't last long. The girl soon decided that Reiner wasn't for her, but her sister, Margot, took a liking to him. They started to go out together. She was then thirty-one years old, quite a bit younger than Reiner, and she suffered some health problems, mainly related to her thyroid gland. This relationship did develop, so much so that the pair got engaged, and the marriage was arranged for the spring of 1963.

There were far more relatives from Margot's family at the wedding than from Reiner's, because it was a double wedding. Margot's sister, the one Reiner had first gone out with, was married at the same time. Those of Reiner's family who attended were Anna, Peter, Inge and Andras from Karlsruhe, and Franz, Victoria and Marika from Kornwestheim. The relatives remaining in Hungary couldn't attend the wedding. The marriage service was held at Margot's father's church in the Pfalz. Margot's father, as was to be expected, conducted the marriage service. As a marriage you would have thought that it should have been a happy affair, but Margot's father made it clear to all the guests that the ceremony was to be a solemn religious affair, and he did not want any laughing or smiling in the church.

In addition to that, he insisted that there was to be no laughing, smiling, music or dancing at the reception. In view of his three marriages and number of children, perhaps he thought that the joys of marriage should be confined to the privacy of the marriage bed. In any case the reception turned out to be quite lively, because there were a number of young children of similar age to Marika there, and it was impossible to keep them still or quiet.

Following the marriage Margot moved in with Reiner and Anna.

॰ॐ

Back in Kornwestheim, Franz was becoming restless at work. He wanted to better himself. He was bored with his life. Victoria never knew at what time he was likely to arrive home from work, because he would often stop off in a café for a coffee. His real reason for doing this was so that he could talk to other people. Once Franz started talking he lost all track of time, and he would always be the last to leave the café. Alcohol was never a big attraction to him, but he was easily intoxicated by the sound of his own voice.

He could not see any opportunity to improve his situation as a fitter, so he enrolled on a course to train to be a draughtsman. He could do the course at home in his spare time. He had to buy a drawing board, and this stood in the corner of the living room. A colleague at work recommended a university student living nearby, who came to the flat to give him lessons in maths. Victoria sat at the table in the living room to watch the lessons, although she didn't take part. She soon realised that Franz wasn't very good at maths, because she could understand the teaching better than he could. Franz was good with his hands, not so good with more complex arithmetic.

He managed to complete the course, and looked around for a job as a draughtsman. He found a job with a local building firm. When he had been there a few months he decided that he was fully proficient at the job, and therefore he ought to receive more pay.

He went to the manager, and said, "I can do the job, but I have to have more pay. Either you give me a raise in pay, or I will have to hand in my notice."

He was a more than a little surprised when the manager immediately accepted his resignation. It was summer 1963.

Victoria was not pleased. Was there no limit to Franz's stupidity? Now the three of them would have to live on her income.

Franz decided he had had enough of working for other people. He wanted his own business, preferably something connected with farming, or land. He came up with the idea of growing flowers. He had looked round the local towns, and realised that there were hardly any shops specifically selling flowers, and that those there were tended to be next to the cemeteries. He reckoned there was a gap in the market for shops in the town centres, and that the local weekly produce markets could support stalls selling flowers, particularly at the weekends. People were becoming more affluent, and would like to buy decorative flowers for their flats. He visited the local open-air markets on the respective market days. There were no stalls selling flowers in the small Kornwestheim market, nor in the larger one at nearby Ludwigsburg. Kornwestheim market days were Wednesday and Friday, the main day in Ludwigsburg was Saturday.

There was a field to rent on the edge of Kornwestheim on the northern side, not too far from the blocks of flats where the family lived. It wasn't big enough for wheat or corn, but Franz reckoned it was just the right size to grow flowers. He went to the centre of Stuttgart, where he knew there was a shop selling flowers. The owner was quite open about how the business was run, and gave Franz some useful tips. Most of the flowers came from Holland, where they were grown under glass in winter. He gave Franz the address of his supplier. Franz made contact with the Dutch supplier, who was able to put him in touch with a producer of flower bulbs.

Franz started to put some figures together. He realised that it was no good renting a field, planting bulbs, and waiting for them to grow. He needed income in the meantime, because it would take all his money to rent the field and buy the bulbs. He could sell flowers on three days in the markets, and still have time to tend the bulbs in the field.

Victoria didn't think much of the idea. She was not a

risk-taker. She needed certainty in her life, but there was no stopping Franz. In this case, for a change, he was right. There was a gap in the market for him to exploit. He soon had the market stalls up and running, and making a profit. He rented the field and took delivery of a huge container of bulbs from Holland. He had to hire some workers to help him plant the bulbs, and to look after them as they grew. He took on two men who lived locally. One day, very soon after he had employed them, one of them was riding to work on his bike, and at the same time drinking beer from a bottle. He fell off the bike, the bottle broke, and he got a nasty gash on his leg. This meant that he was off work sick for several weeks almost as soon as he had started. Franz was now an employer, and had to pay the man's wages whilst he was off work sick. Franz began to realise that being in business wasn't as straightforward as he thought.

Soon he was becoming very busy. The car wasn't practical for the business, and had to go. He changed it for an estate car, with plenty of space in the back to carry the flowers. Victoria had learnt to drive, so she could help when necessary. She had to help him after her work and at weekends. Marika helped out on the market stall on a Saturday. Franz found an old disused barn to rent, not far from the flat and close to the centre of town, to use as a store for the flowers. On the evening before each market day he and Victoria went there to prepare bouquets and flower bunches for sale on the market stalls. The stalls became very busy, particularly the Saturday one at Ludwigsburg. Franz and Victoria would often be at the barn preparing up to three a.m. on a Saturday morning, and then be at the market stall for seven a.m. the same morning. It was very hard work, particularly for Victoria, who was still working at the shoe factory, doing the housework, shopping, and cooking.

Marika saw little of her parents during this period. They seemed always to be working. When school was finished she went to the kindergarten.

One day, early in the summer of 1964, Marika was surprised when her mother arrived at the kindergarten early from work. Her mother, Anna, had died suddenly at home in Karlsruhe. It was not clear what she had died of. The doctor put it down to a heart attack, though Anna had not shown previous symptoms. Since Anna had rarely visited the doctor there had not been much evidence to go on. If she was suffering she had kept it to herself. She was sixty-four. It was many years later, after both Reiner and Victoria were diagnosed with diabetes, that the family wondered if Anna had been suffering from diabetes, never diagnosed, from which she had died.

The next few days seemed like a blur to Marika. She had not experienced a family death before. She had been very close to her grandmother, and thought she should experience sadness and tears, but it didn't register with her that way. Victoria had to go to buy black clothes for the funeral. She would follow the old tradition and wear black for one year after her mother's death.

The family went to the funeral in Karlsruhe. First they went to Anna's flat, and then to the cemetery. Here tradition was followed, with the coffin remaining open for people to pay their respects. Marika hated the open coffin, and kept well away. The funeral was well attended. Anna had lots of friends locally amongst the neighbours, and she was still regarded as "Mother Hungary", so lots of people who had been refugees were there.

If there had been a will Victoria was never shown it. There were few physical possessions, but there were some savings. Victoria received a very small amount. She believed, rightly or wrongly, that her brothers had shared out most of what there was between themselves.

Following Anna's death, Reiner and Margot continued to live in the flat. Margot twice became pregnant, but each time she suffered a miscarriage.

ℭ

It was becoming easier to travel to Hungary. Reiner and Margot went several times to visit Reiner's relatives in the Kismányok area. They were able to take holidays there. Hungary, like Germany, had spa towns, where it was possible to book in for a week or more to take "the cure". This usually comprised of the local waters, rich in minerals of one kind or another, but the rest of the facilities provided were excellent. The Communists hadn't got rid of the spas. They counted as part of the country's health provision, but in addition the Party hierarchy liked to take advantage of the facilities for themselves and their families. Foreigners were allowed to pay to visit the spas. Those in Hungary were a good deal cheaper to attend than the ones in Germany, because Hungarians simply didn't have the money to pay German prices. Visitors could stay with local families in the spa towns; accommodation was very basic, but cheap. The locals were glad of any extra income. This suited Reiner, who was always very cautious when it came to spending his money. He saved as much as he could, because he hoped that one day he and Margot would be able to buy a small flat. Besides, he loved to go back to his native Hungary, and the holiday allowed him to visit his relatives. Of all the refugees in our story, it was Reiner who continued to miss the land of his birth the most. Often, when he visited his brother Peter, they would talk in Hungarian about the old times of their childhoods and youth in Hungary.

෧

Franz's father, Josef, still lived in Kornwestheim. Sometimes Franz would pass him in the street, but most of the time Josef would ignore him or look away. He wouldn't acknowledge his own son. Just occasionally, on a good day Josef might nod in his direction. Josef was by the middle 'sixties a pensioner, but he had never earned, or worked regularly enough to become entitled to a decent pension. Franz, as his only son, was required to contribute to his father's pension. Franz was obliged to provide financial support for his father, who refused to speak to him. It's a strange world.

Franz was becoming more ambitious. Even Victoria could see that the flower-growing and selling was making money, so it wasn't difficult for Franz to persuade Victoria to give up her job to help him. She just couldn't cope with two jobs and a home to run. His next idea was to open shops to sell flowers for the whole week, not just on market days. He could see himself as the owner of a huge flower-selling business with a shop in every town in the area. Victoria's cautious nature was evident.

"You can't employ staff in shops where you aren't there to control them. They will rob you from the takings."

The difference in their view of human nature was obvious.

"Of course not," replied Franz. "You think everyone is out to rob you. Most people are honest."

"Well, we'll see," thought Victoria.

Franz saw some miniature daffodils in a shop. He thought they looked unusual, and would be a good seller, but how to grow them? Then he had an idea. After planting a row of daffodil bulbs in the field he went down the row and firmed the soil over each bulb with his heel so that it was quite hard. He kept it firm until the shoots started to show. He was delighted to see that the daffodils grew smaller than the normal crop, and miniature daffodils became a good seller.

He continued to employ the two men in the field caring for the growing flowers. Then he had another of his little brainwaves. At the end of every week he would invite the workmen to come to the flat for dinner and to drink some beer, as a "thank you" for their hard work. He didn't tell Victoria about this until he had asked them. So Victoria found herself working until three o'clock in the morning Friday through Saturday helping Franz prepare flowers for market. Then she was working on the stall from seven a.m. until after three p.m. Then she had to go home to start preparing an evening meal for five people. When Franz and his workmen arrived they sat around drinking beer until the meal was ready. The men had big appetites and Victoria had to cook in quantity in the tiny kitchen. Needless to say she didn't think much of her Saturday chores.

The first flower shop was opened in Kornwestheim, near to the station. In 1964, Eva had retired from her job at the canteen, and Franz asked her to look after the shop. She was happy to do so. She was good with money, and loved being involved with anything that made a profit. The shop was a success.

Franz was looking to expand. His dream of a chain of flower shops all over the region was within reach, or so he thought. Stuttgart itself was a large prospering city, and there were numerous sizeable towns around, all of which he thought could support shops. Victoria, as usual, was much more cautious, and told him once again, "You will over stretch yourself. These are cash businesses, and you don't know enough people whom you can trust. The staff will rob you, because you can't check on them all the time."

Franz dismissed her views. Nobody would ever do any trade if they listened to people like her.

❧

By the early 'sixties social changes were beginning to rock the old established unwritten rules and people's attitudes. The changes had begun to impact at the end of the Second World War, but the long re-building process had delayed their impact. Now, in the 'sixties, a degree of prosperity was growing amongst all levels of society in the western world. A new youth culture was refusing to comply with old ways. A major feature of the new culture was music aimed at and performed by the young. Many of the singers and musicians were without any formal training. The music had developed in the mid 'fifties in America, from a mixture of blues and dance band music, but with many other influences such as country and jazz. The sounds soon crossed the Atlantic to Europe, where, without the originating influences, they developed into simple pop songs sung to a rock-and-roll dance beat. Then in 1963 Europe took over as the driving force in teenage music. The Beatles, and others like them, pushed forward the boundaries of the music. The musicians became heroes of youth. When the pop stars turned to using drugs as a form of recreation, the youth of Western countries copied them. The introduction of the contraceptive pill for women helped to change sexual attitudes. Sex outside of marriage became the norm, and acceptable to those growing up in these times of change.

To those who were a little older, the changes came too late to change their attitudes, since they had grown up before or during the war. They may have looked on in envy at the new freedoms, but for most of the slightly older generation they just passed them by. Franz and Victoria were now both in their thirties. They appreciated the new music, but drug culture was not for them. They went to see the first James Bond film, *Dr No*, and talked about it for hours afterwards. The sexual morality and callous violence expressed in the film as entertainment was something they had never seen depicted before.

There were changes in the workplaces too. Labour in the form of trade unions exercised its power, and few employers or governments could stand up against it. Employees achieved pay and benefit improvements that would have been impossible dreams fifteen years earlier. There were jobs for everyone, and many employees working in heavy unionised workplaces didn't have to work hard to get excellent pay. Ordinary workers could afford to buy televisions and cars. They could go on package holidays to the sunspots of the Mediterranean, and beyond. Germany was at the forefront of this growing prosperity. There was a big difference between West Germany and the East. In the West the market economy expanded very quickly, and everyone received the benefit. In the East everyone had a job, but many factories were inefficient, with little or no capital investment being made. Wages were low in the East, and there were few goods to buy in the shops. The Communist countries bought and sold to each other at agreed fixed prices, which often bore no relationship to the costs of production. In fairness to the Communist states of Eastern Europe, investment was maintained in healthcare and in schools, and emphasis was placed on sports achievements. It was important to display the success of Communism to the rest of the world, and for relatively small financial outlay it was possible to do that in sport. Unfortunately there were other areas requiring massive investment, such as weapons development, and the exploration of outer space, which Russia and its allies undertook in order to maintain the image of superiority, or at least equality, with the capitalist West.

Marika was growing up in a totally different world to that which her parents had experienced. In 1965, at the age of eleven, she took the school tests, which would determine the rest of her school education. She passed the tests with good results, which meant that in September she started at the highest level secondary school in Kornwestheim, the Ernst-Siegle-Gymnasium. She was already into the Beatlemania phase. She bought one of the very few records of their English hits to be recorded by them also in German, "Sie liebt dich" ("She Loves You").

Her relationships with her parents were different. Franz had not shown much interest in what Marika was doing when she was very young. Perhaps this was nothing particularly against her, though he had regarded her as the reason for his having to get married too young. Maybe it was just his nature, or a result of his own upbringing with a harsh father, and a cold, unaffectionate mother. The truth was that he rarely showed much interest in other people, asked them how they were, or what they were doing. He talked a lot, but people who do that tend to be repetitive, and the talk is usually of their own experiences, views and achievements. There are a lot of people around like that.

Marika was closer to her mother, but, for as long as Marika could remember, Victoria had talked to her and treated her on adult terms. Victoria had inherited her own mother's sense of humour to some extent, which meant that it didn't take much to make her laugh, but she had rarely played children's games with Marika. There had never been much in the way of toys, but Franz and Victoria had bought board games, and the three of them spent many evenings playing these together. Marika could play with toys belonging to the other children she knew. Since her parents were so busy during her early teenage years, Marika spent a lot of time on her own or with friends.

Franz and Victoria were very keen for Marika to do well at school, and they were delighted when she passed the test at age eleven. Franz remembered the difficulties he had suffered due to his father's attempts to stop him doing his schoolwork, and Victoria had never continued her education following the family leaving Hungary, when she was just thirteen years old. Marika was not a problem child, and her parents never had to worry about her behaviour.

## Chapter Eleven

OVER THE NEXT two years Franz opened two more flower shops, one in a nearby part of Stuttgart, almost a large town on its own, and not far from Kornwestheim, the other close to the centre of Stuttgart itself. He asked his mother to staff the one in the centre. He reasoned it would become the busiest shop, and, since it was furthest away from Kornwestheim, he thought she would be the best person to run it, without his having to go there every day to supervise. That meant he had to find staff for the other two shops. He found a woman to look after the newer shop, and two to staff the one in Kornwestheim, which had become quite busy.

After the initial opening periods the new shops settled down to regular patterns of sales. The only thing was that the one in Kornwestheim, and the new one in the nearby suburb of Stuttgart didn't seem to be making profit. The one staffed by Eva did well.

Franz reasoned that he needed to show the new staff how to sell flowers. They just needed to see how he did it. So he spent time working in each shop so that the staff would learn. When he worked in a shop the takings improved, but once he left it to the staff they fell again.

Franz and Victoria had different explanations for the situation.

"I told you that you can't trust staff. They are robbing you and you can't see it."

"No, don't be silly. You can't expect them to be as good at selling as I am. They will get better in time."

Time went on, and the shops' takings didn't improve. Franz and Victoria continued to argue the reasons, but neither would alter their view.

Marika noticed that her parents were arguing more. It was difficult to avoid it in the confines of the flat. She thought it was because of the stresses of running the flower business.

What she didn't know, at first, was that Victoria thought that Franz was having an affair with one of the women that worked in the Kornwestheim shop. He was coming home later most evenings, and when she challenged him he said that he had more work to do to try to make the shops profitable.

This went on for some time early in 1968. Finally, one evening Victoria decided she would go see for herself where Franz was. She left Marika at the flat and went to the shop in Kornwestheim. It was in darkness. She then went to the flats where she knew one of the women staff at the shop lived. Parked outside the flats was Franz's estate car. That was it. Her suspicions were confirmed. She knew the woman was a divorcee, and could think of no valid reason why Franz should be there at that time. She waited a good half-hour to see if Franz returned to the car. There was no sign of him, but she could see that the light was on in the woman's flat. She walked back home.

When Franz returned home there was a very long and loud argument between the couple in the flat. Marika went to her bedroom and trembled as she listened to it all. Victoria was not prepared to listen to Franz's feeble excuses. As far as she was concerned the marriage was over. There would be no going back. She wanted a divorce.

Franz would have to sleep in the small bedroom until he had somewhere else to go. Victoria and Marika slept in the main bedroom.

Victoria was not going to carry on working for Franz in the flower business. She went to the shoe factory, and they offered her a job. She didn't care what Franz did. She wanted him out of the flat and divorced as soon as possible.

Franz continued to live at the flat for a while, but he and Victoria started to lead separate lives.

When summer came, Victoria decided she needed to get away for a holiday. She decided she would go to Hungary with Marika. This would be the first time Victoria had been back since she had fled with her mother and brother more than twenty years earlier. She told Franz that she was going to go in the car. After all, she considered it as much hers as his. She told him he should check the car over to make sure everything was in working order. She also asked him to put a film in the camera, which she was taking with her. Franz agreed to make these preparations.

It was going to be a long drive. The roads were motorways in Germany, and part of Austria, but got worse the further east they went. Victoria and Marika set off at three a.m. in the morning. Before they had got to Munich they had a flat tyre. Victoria went for the spare tyre, and found that it was totally bald. She got out the car jack, and the tools to take off the wheel. She got a shock, because the nuts on the wheel were loose. She could take them off using her fingers. She was livid. She was convinced that Franz had deliberately left the nuts loose, and that he was trying to kill both of them.

She bought a new tyre for the spare, and they carried on. In Austria the fan belt snapped. Victoria was now totally convinced that Franz had not checked the car at all, and that he had deliberately loosened the wheel nuts.

They found somewhere to stay overnight near Vienna, and carried on the following morning to the Hungarian border. Here every vehicle was stopped and searched before being allowed to continue. The roads in Hungary were not so good so it was late in the afternoon when they reached Kismányok. Victoria drove carefully along the narrow track to the farmhouse at the end of the village, where Hartmut and Maria Nagy still lived.

The house was very crowded. Hartmut's father was still alive. Hartmut and Maria's son and daughter, now in their late teens, still lived there. There were other visitors staying. A female cousin of Victoria and Maria had come from East Germany with her two teenage daughters. All of these, plus Victoria and Marika had to sleep in three quite small rooms. To the three teenage girls this was fine. They got on well with each other.

On the second morning after their arrival there was a shock. Hartmut had to announce that his father had died in his sleep. There was little sadness shown for the death of the old man. He was totally unloved. Hartmut and Maria believed his unreasonable behaviour had driven Hartmut's mother to suicide some years earlier.

There was turmoil, because, despite the presence of all the visitors, a funeral had to be arranged. There was little money to pay for anything for the funeral. The family had always lived off the land, being almost self-sufficient. They were one of the few families remaining in Kismányok who still lived in that way. The Hungarians who had taken over the houses following the expulsion of the Germans after the end of the war were working families, but they weren't prepared to work from dawn until dusk 365 days a year as subsistence farmers. They worked for farms, or travelled by bus to factory jobs in the nearby large town of Bonyhád. Hartmut and Maria clung to a way of life that had almost disappeared.

Victoria agreed to allow the estate car to be used as a hearse. It was only a couple of hundred metres to the church and the cemetery. Within two days the old man was buried, with religious ceremony, but few, if any, tears.

There was one relative it was important for Victoria to visit, her mother's sister, Aunt Eva, who had taken Victoria in more than twenty years earlier, after the police had boarded up the door to the house in Nagymányok. She still lived in Vasas, near Pécs, with one of her grown-up daughters, now married to a Hungarian. She insisted in speaking Hungarian.

It was an emotional reunion, especially as Victoria's mother, Anna, wasn't there to be part of it. Victoria had retained her skill in speaking Hungarian, so there wasn't a problem, though Marika could understand only a little of what was being said.

The visit meant a drive from Nagymányok to Pécs. Victoria's nerves were in a bad state. In addition to the problems at home with Franz, the stresses of all that had happened on the journey and since their arrival in Hungary had affected her state of mind. She was an inexperienced driver and had never undertaken such a long journey by car before. Whilst driving in the busy city of Pécs Victoria's car was in a collision with a motorcycle. The man on the bike fell off, but he wasn't injured, and his old bike had just another scratch added to its collection. He wasn't in a rage over the accident. This was a lucky escape for Victoria, because if the biker had reported the incident she could have been put into jail.

After a few more days staying with Hartmut and Maria, both sets of visitors decided they would like to go to Lake Balaton for a short holiday before leaving for home. They all went in Victoria's car, and found a chalet to stay in close to the Lake.

The weather wasn't kind. It rained and was cold for the time of year. Despite this, Marika remembered the few days there with pleasure. The two women and three teenage girls had a really good time together.

On the return journey Victoria and Marika found the border to Austria blocked with lines of Russian tanks. All vehicles were diverted and delayed because of thorough searches being made by soldiers. It was the time of the Russian invasion of Czechoslovakia, and security had been tightened up considerably in all the Eastern Block satellite countries. Victoria remembered the time when she, her mother, and Reiner had been turned off the train as they tried to flee to Germany all those years before. This time there was a long delay, but eventually they were allowed to cross into Austria without difficulty.

The rest of the return journey to Kornwestheim passed, thankfully, without incident.

By the time they got home Victoria had worked up a fury. She accused Franz of deliberately trying to kill them both by leaving the wheel nuts loose.

Franz denied it. It was just an oversight on his part.

The following day Victoria decided to take the film from the camera to the shop for processing. She opened the camera to find that there was no film inside.

If there had ever been any faint hope of a reconciliation between Franz and Victoria it had been finally killed off by the events of the Hungarian trip.

Soon afterwards Franz moved out to live with his new girlfriend for a while. Divorce proceedings took their slow course.

෯

Over in Karlsruhe Margot had a baby boy in September 1968. Now each of Anna's children had one child. Each child of the new generation had been born in Germany.

෯

The year 1968, like most of the 'sixties, had seen turmoil around the world, much of it evidenced by violent events. Martin Luther King was assassinated. There were race riots in America. Robert Kennedy met his death in the same way that his brother had done five years earlier, at the hands of a gunman. The Vietnam War continued apace, despite the signs of growing opposition by sections of the American public. Alexander Dubcek, the new Czech leader tried to bring about reforms to the Communist system in his country, only to find that the Russians would send in tanks to stop the changes. Students rioted in Paris. Bloody wars and massacres of civilians were taking place in southern Africa. Manned spacecraft orbited the moon, as the USA prepared to land a human there for the first time. Arthur Ashe became the first black man to win the US Tennis Open, and the first black woman was elected to the House of Representatives in the USA. Looking back on these events they seemed to depict a battle to change the established world order on many fronts at the same time, fought against by those frightened of change, who would do anything to prevent, or at least delay it.

## Chapter Twelve

AT THIS POINT our story should come to an end, but, being a true story, of course it doesn't. The families in our story, forced out of their Hungarian homeland in the aftermath of war, had made new lives in Germany. They were able to take part in, and benefit from, the economic miracle that was the re-generation of Germany after the Second World War.

Peter and Inge moved twice in Karlsruhe, eventually living in a rented top floor flat in a large building. Over the years they accumulated a sizeable amount of money, but it was never clear to the rest of the family quite how they managed to do that. Peter was, after all, just a chauffeur, and Inge never worked more than part-time. They maintained American friends, and the family always believed that Peter was involved with things that might not have been totally above board, but it was all conjecture. Their son, Andras, became an administrator, married, and adopted his wife's son. Peter and Inge were able to buy a flat for Andras, who continued to live in Karlsruhe.

After Peter's retirement the couple lived quietly together in their flat. Early in 1996 Peter had a mild stroke. This affected his speech, but Inge didn't realise he was ill. She thought he was trying to speak to her in Hungarian, which she couldn't understand. It was two days before she called Reiner, who came round to see Peter, realised there was a problem, and called in medical help. From then on Peter's health gradually deteriorated, and he died later the same year. The rest of the family had thought that Inge's behaviour had become strange, but it was some time after Peter's death that she was diagnosed as suffering from dementia, and she had to go to live in a home.

❦

Soon after the birth of their son, Manfred in 1968, Reiner and Margot moved into a ground-floor flat, which they were buying. Reiner continued to work as a carpenter, and Margot worked in an accounts office in Karlsruhe. Reiner always missed Hungary more than his brother and sister. He was the one who made the most visits to Kismányok, the village of his birth. Their son, Manfred, grew to be exceptionally tall, just over two metres. He went to university to study geology, but it was almost the new millennium before he was to leave his parents' home for good to live in Frankfurt, where, having achieved a doctorate, he started a job with an American-owned firm.

Reiner's health began to fail by the year 2000. He had a slowly developing prostate cancer, but in 2002 was suffering from cancer in other parts of his body, and he died that October. Margot continued to live alone in the flat. She kept in contact with her stepbrothers and her sisters from her father's various marriages. She also kept in touch with Victoria in Kornwestheim, and with Marika in England, by telephone.

ɕ

Franz soon split with his girlfriend in 1968, but then took up with the other shop assistant in his Kornwestheim shop. She was divorced, and had two young daughters. They set up home together, and Franz had a son by her. The couple never married, which meant that his son took the mother's surname.

Franz gradually realised that his business dreams were never going to come true. One by one the shops were closed, until he was left with his market stalls, and selling flowers from his barn store on Sunday mornings. He made a living, but he was never good with money, so didn't save. This meant, being self-employed, his pension entitlement wasn't much, so he carried on working after he should have retired.

Eva, his mother, still retained her in-bred financial toughness. She had saved something regularly ever since she had worked in Germany. Using the money she received as compensation for the lost lands in Hungary, and her savings made over the years, Eva bought a house in Kornwestheim. Franz and his new family lived downstairs, whilst Eva lived upstairs. Franz's father died in 1973. Eva, although she had been divorced for many years, paid for a plot for his burial in the local cemetery. Eva had a fall in her flat early in 1988. She couldn't move, and the doctor was called. He diagnosed severe bruising and said she would recover with rest. She was still in severe pain more than a week later, so Franz called the doctor again. It was finally realised that Eva's thigh was broken. Following that incident her health deteriorated steadily and she died in the autumn of 1988. She had left instructions that she was to be buried in the same plot as her ex-husband. Being a good Catholic she was determined that, even though she had parted from her husband in life, in death they would stay together.

Franz inherited the house. His mother had bought a small piece of land cheaply, as an investment, which was about ten miles from Kornwestheim. The land was on a slope, and apart from yielding a few apples, was not a profitable investment. Following his mother's death Franz sold the land, and used the proceeds to buy a new van for his business. During the 1990s Franz's woman-friend left him to live with another man. Franz remained on good terms with the woman's daughters, who had both married, but still lived nearby. His son lived with Franz on and off. He seemed to have inherited Franz's restless nature, moving from job to job, without settling to a career.

ॐ

Once the divorce from Franz had been finalised, Victoria and Marika continued to live in the same flat in Kornwestheim. Marika grew quite tall, and she allowed her dark hair to grow long, so that it almost reached her waist at the back. She was a good scholar, and liked languages in particular. Following her final year in the sixth form at the Gymnasium she went to university in Freiburg, where she read English and French. Victoria couldn't offer much support financially, so Marika often took jobs to help support herself. She also used the student loan system. There was no time pressure to complete a course at a German university, so it was some years before Marika felt that she was ready to leave and look for work. She liked the student life, and was happy to live in Freiburg, where she had several boyfriends. She took a teacher-training course to complete her time at university. When this was finished she found that there was a surplus of teachers in Germany, and not enough jobs for newly trained entrants. In any case, she had come to dislike the regimented way of life in Germany.

After some deliberation she decided to look for work in England. She found a job as a language assistant at a school in Leeds in the north of England. She gradually built up sufficient assignments teaching German to English students at various colleges in the Leeds district, and eventually found a full-time position as a lecturer in Leeds.

In 1985 she was thirty-one years old, and decided that it was time to adopt a different hairstyle, so she had her long, dark hair trimmed right back. She met a man ten years older than herself, and they set up home in Leeds together in 1988.

That was where I entered the story, because my name is David Bridges, I am that man, and you are now reading my work.

At the age of forty-two, in 1985, I had decided to start a course in German at evening class at the local college. Marika was taking the class. At the time I considered myself to be happily married, living with my wife, teenage son and daughter, in a pleasant house in a suburb on the outskirts of Leeds. I was preparing to settle into middle age without expecting any emotional problems. Such stresses as I had were in my job as an accountant and administrator with a fast-growing small company. I had never dreamed of another romance to come.

The first year of the German course passed, starting in September 1985 and ending in June 1986. At the beginning of 1986 my father was diagnosed as having cancer. The last few months up to his death early in August 1986 were harrowing and stressful for all our family.

To be honest, I don't think I had given Marika a second thought. I had hardly noticed her in the midst of all the stressful events of the time. Then, suddenly, whilst we were on a family holiday in Austria in late August 1986, I found that I was thinking about Marika. I wasn't lusting after her, just thinking about her, and the more I tried to put her out of my mind, the more she was invading my waking thoughts. I could not believe what was happening to me.

I enrolled for the second year of the German course in September 1986. From then on I paid much more attention to Marika. Some of the class started to go to a nearby pub after the class, including Marika, and I joined them. We chatted during these brief meetings, and I began to find out about her life. I am sure that the other people from the class going to the pub could see that there was an attraction between the two of us, probably more than we were able to identify at first.

My wife had also realised that my behaviour had changed, and our relationship was becoming difficult. Marika and I started meeting secretly, usually at lunchtimes, since we were working within a couple of miles of each other. When we met we just talked. There was no sex at that stage of our relationship. My wife realised that there was someone else in my life and we had a number of arguments. She couldn't understand why I wanted to break up a happy marriage after so many years. I couldn't explain my feelings, but knew I had to go to Marika. Finally my wife forced a confrontation between the three of us. I was forced to make a choice between the two of them. For a few days I tried to put Marika out of my head, and save my marriage, but it was not going to work, and I knew it. I decided to give up my old life, to leave my home, and find a flat. In April 1987 I moved into a two-room flat in an old terrace house not far from Leeds University. Marika moved into another flat nearby. In February 1988 we took out a loan to buy a house together in Leeds.

My life now changed completely. I joined Marika on her visits to Kornwestheim to stay with Victoria in her flat.

๙

Following Marika's departure for England in 1981 Victoria continued to live alone in the flat. She began to suffer health problems as she grew older. One of her knees became painful, and she had to have an operation to remove part of the bone. She was diagnosed as diabetic, which meant she had to change her diet completely. She would have to take various pills on a daily basis for the rest of her life.

Ever since her divorce Victoria's cynical view of people had grown further, to the extent that she believed someone who appeared to do something nice always had an ulterior motive. If she spoke about her marriage, or Franz, it seemed she believed that he had committed a great crime against her. Yet sometimes, at Christmas, when Marika and I visited from England, Franz would be invited to the flat for a family dinner. Then, just occasionally, when Franz and Victoria talked, it seemed as if the years dropped away, and there was a spark of what had once been.

Victoria worked at the shoe factory until her retirement. Gradually the manufacture of shoes was transferred from the Kornwestheim factory. The manufacturers couldn't afford to continue to pay German rates to their workers, so production was moved to countries, mostly in Eastern Europe, where pay levels were much lower. By the year 2000 all shoe manufacture had ceased in Kornwestheim. The huge factory was re-developed as a retail shopping centre, though part of the buildings remain in use as the administrative headquarters for the manufacturing group, and one of the retail units is for the sale of shoes made within the group.

Victoria became somewhat reclusive. She kept in touch with her brothers in Karlsruhe, though more with Reiner than with Peter. Sometimes they would visit each other by car, though Victoria was never keen on driving, and usually kept to the few routes in Kornwestheim and nearby Ludwigsburg, which she was used to. Apart from a few work colleagues she didn't have many friends. She spoke to Marika in England by telephone at least once each week, and visited England for holidays on several occasions.

The inhabitants of the block of flats where Victoria lived

had all been refugees. In the German tradition they regarded these flats as their permanent homes, so they stayed there. They had children who grew up and moved away. Gradually the older residents began to die off. Most of the flats were becoming occupied by immigrant families, from Italy, Turkey, Jugoslavia, Greece, Portugal, or similar, who were allocated these flats by the council on arrival in the area. Attitudes to these immigrants varied. Some of the inhabitants, particularly in southern Germany, seemed to have forgotten that they themselves had once arrived in the country as refugees with nothing. Present-day Germans didn't want the flats. They were too small, and the facilities were out of date. I noticed that over the years following my first visit to Kornwestheim in 1987 the number of immigrant families in Kornwestheim, and particularly in the council flats where Victoria lived, grew considerably.

The wall, which had divided West from East Berlin for forty years, was demolished in 1989. Following more than forty years as two separate states, Germany was re-united. Old-style Russian and East European Communism was dead, imploded under its own economic impossibilities.

Following re-unification and the collapse of Communism in Eastern Europe, those countries that had maintained large numbers of troops in Western Germany since the end of the Second World War, closed down most of their barracks. The land and buildings vacated became available for re-developments. The blocks of flats where Victoria had lived since 1956 had always been overlooked on one side by the huge blank wall of an American barracks. By the year 2000 the Americans had gone. The barracks were demolished. A large area was cleared for new housing. It was a prime site, convenient for the centre of Kornwestheim, and close to the main road joining Stuttgart and Ludwigsburg.

Sometimes, when Marika and I visited Germany, Victoria, her brother Reiner, and Franz would talk about their lives in Hungary, and how they had come to Germany after the Second World War. They couldn't speak English, but gradually, over a period of several years, and with Marika's help, I managed to piece together their stories.

There was no way I could check on their individual experiences, so I had to hope that their recollections of events, some of which had taken place fifty years or more earlier, were accurate.

I was able to verify the major events by carrying out research into the history of Hungary and Germany over a long period. The families' experiences fitted the historical facts. I decided to write down their stories. Most of what you are reading is a true account, as told to me by those who lived through the events. Just occasionally I have used some "poetic licence" in order to provide continuity to the story, where I was not able to ascertain the detail. It is sad, that since both Reiner and Peter Moser are both now dead, I can't ask them for more corroboration.

# Chapter Thirteen

WHAT BECAME OF the relatives in Hungary?

In August 1997 Marika and I flew to Budapest from England. We met Victoria, who had flown from Stuttgart, at the airport. We stayed for a few days in Budapest, exploring the ancient city.

We hired a car and drove to the town of Gyula, in the south-eastern corner of Hungary, right on the Rumanian border. We had arranged to stay in a holiday cottage there for a few days. Gyula is a large town, about five miles from the village of Elek.

We drove to Elek, and parked close to the church in the centre. It was a hot summer's day, and very little stirred in the village centre. We walked around the streets, still maintained in their grid layout, as designed and constructed over 250 years previously by the German settlers. Many of the houses were small single-storey dwellings. It was difficult to tell their age. There was little evidence of any large-scale building projects carried out in the Communist era.

An old lady pushing a bicycle saw us standing by the church wall, and came up to us. She spoke to us in German, though Marika said afterwards that the dialect she spoke was not any modern one. She asked if we were looking for anything. Victoria and Marika explained who we were, and why we were there. Victoria asked the lady if she knew any survivors of the Sellner family. She said that she thought there had been two families in Elek that she could remember of that name, but didn't think that any were now still living.

Marika asked the lady if she was of German descent.

She replied, "Yes. I should have left Elek on one of the trains to Germany in 1946. My name was on the list, but my grandparents hid me until it was safe for me to re-appear. I was born here, and have lived all my life in Elek."

ॐ

From Gyula we drove across the south of Hungary to the Pécs area. We had arranged to stay in a wooden holiday cabin not far from the town of Komló, mid way between Pécs and Kismányok.

We visited Vasas, on the outskirts of Pécs to see Victoria's Aunt Eva, who had looked after her for a time following the eviction from the flat in Nagymányok, so many years previously. Eva was now an old lady, but still seemed fit and well. She had long since given up speaking German. Those days were long gone. She was Hungarian, and there was no point in looking backwards. She occupied the ground floor of the house in Vasas. Her daughter lived on the floors above with her Hungarian husband, grown-up son and daughter. They could speak only Hungarian, so it was a good job that Victoria still retained her fluency in the language.

We drove to Nagymányok. We parked our car and walked around the part of the village where Victoria had lived with her mother, father, and brothers. The house where she was born was still there and in use. The nearby mine where her father had worked was still operating. We walked along the lanes close to the hill separating that part of Nagymányok from Kismányok. Victoria took us along a lane to look at the plot of land the family had once owned, where they had grown corn to feed the pigs. Part of the field now had houses built on it.

We took the road round the hillside into the valley containing the village of Kismányok. We passed the church and followed the single-track road round to the end of the village to the last house on the left, that belonging to Hartmut and Maria Nagy. As we entered the yard we could see that Maria was working in the shed to our right, bottling fruit for the winter, exactly as she had done for so many years.

We were invited into the kitchen/dining/living room. We ate a meal of chicken. Then Maria produced a large plate containing a huge pile of home-made individual strudel pastries. I can honestly say that I have never tasted anything like them. Hartmut said that Maria had been up since five a.m. preparing the food for our visit. There were far too many for us to eat.

Hartmut showed us the house. The two connecting bedrooms looked as if they had been unchanged for many years. Outside there were two large pigs in their fairly small pen. It looked as if it would not be long before they would be slaughtered to provide meat for winter. We used the toilet outside. There was now running water for the house, but the toilet was still an old earth closet.

Hartmut and Maria were now both quite old. Maria had difficulty walking. They both spoke German.

Hartmut invited us to walk up the hillside with him. It was a hot and sunny August afternoon. As the track approached the ridge of the low hill we turned left. Here Hartmut had a small piece of land, where peppers and vegetables were growing.

From there we turned in the other direction across the hillside. It was grassland, the grass yellowing in the summer sun. We walked for perhaps three hundred yards around the hillside. There it was, sticking out like a sore thumb, surrounded by the grassland on all sides, Hartmut's vineyard and fruit plot. The other plots had long ago been sold by their owners to a farmer for sheep rearing, but Hartmut had stayed put, determined that, so long as he was able, he would continue the old way of life. The rectangular plot stood on the sloping hillside, and was fenced off to keep the sheep out. Inside the plot was intensively farmed. Rows of vines, together with apricot bushes and other fruit trees ripened in the summer sun. Hartmut gave us ripe apricots to eat, straight from the trees. At one side, about halfway up the plot was the tiny box-like cabin, where Hartmut could rest, eat a snack, or shelter from the rain.

We walked back along the track, and paused at one point so that I could take a photograph of the village of Kismányok nestling in the bottom of the valley below. I suddenly felt an overwhelming nostalgia as I stood there looking down on the village. This was very strange, because this wasn't my country, or my history. Perhaps I realised that I was observing the last remnant of a story that had started almost three hundred years earlier, and that it would not be long before a way of life, and its story, would be gone. I didn't say anything, nor did the others. This was their story, their lives, and perhaps they were too closely involved in it to experience the same feelings.

As we walked back down the track to the bottom of the hill Hartmut stopped to unlock the door to his "cave" in the side of the earth bank. Inside were three large vats containing maturing wine, together with his equipment needed to make it. Hartmut drew off some glasses of wine for us to taste. Each was different, because he grew several varieties of grapes on his plot. The wine was just about ready for consumption, and tasted wonderful.

Maria gave us some of the left-over strudel to take away with us. We were also given a large sausage made from their own pigs, and some paprika made from the peppers growing on their plot at the top of the hillside.

From there we went to visit Maria's daughter, who lived in the village below the church. She was married to a Hungarian, and they had teenage children. Maria's daughter worked in the shoe factory in the town of Bonyhád. She and her husband helped Hartmut and Maria in looking after their land and the vineyard.

Hartmut and Maria are probably part of a very small number of people trying to maintain their German culture and way of life in Hungary. When they are gone the culture will probably disappear with them. Perhaps that is how it should be, although there is evidence in many countries of the world that immigrant populations are able to keep their own cultures and traditions. Since Germans had been defeated in two world wars, hatred towards them continued for many years afterwards, by which time hardly any trace of their culture remained in the countries of Eastern Europe.

It is not possible to change history, but we can reflect on what might have been under different circumstances. If Anna Moser had agreed to change the family name to a Hungarian version, and allowed Reiner to take up a career in the mine, the family might never have gone to Germany. Victoria would never have met Franz, Marika would not have been born, and I would not have written their story. But that is all conjecture, and it is pointless.

၅

Most of this small family of Germans, born in Hungary, were forced out of the land where they were born. They started new lives in Germany, reversing the process of what happened to their ancestors more than 200 years earlier. The wheel turned full circle. Very few of those relatives remaining in Hungary continue to try to retain their German language and culture. When the present generation dies it is likely the culture will die too.

One hopes that the children of the generation born in Hungary and their descendants will never have to experience the dangerous, life-threatening situations endured by their parents and grandparents. The story of the families goes on, but it is a different story, taking place in a very different and ever changing world.